'From Cotton Mills
To Lakeland Hills'

Holiday Cottage in
Lake District 1930s

By Keith Holland

Published by Helm Press

HELM
PRESS

Dedicated to my family

Published by Helm Press
10 Abbey Gardens, Natland, Kendal, Cumbria LA9 7SP

Tel: 015395 61321

E.Mail: HelmPress@natland.freeserve.co.uk

First Published 2005

ISBN 0 9550823 0 7

Typeset and printed by Stramongate Press Ltd

Front cover: Textile Mill, Radcliffe in 1900s – *Radcliffe Local History Society*
Hartbarrow Cottage
Back cover: Keith Holland

Contents

Keith enjoying retirement

Introduction

Although many of the incidents I have written about in this book took place many years ago in the days of pounds, shillings and pence, ration books and accumulator powered wireless sets, they probably were the best years anyone could have chosen to have lived in. Life was a little slower and people had more time for each other, even though they had little in the way of conveniences and comforts as most people have these days.

Life has changed so much in such a relatively short space of time it's almost like living in another world, as many people of my generation will agree. One only has to push a few buttons to contact somebody on the other side of the world or discover valuable information on the Internet. For this reason I am indebted to three nephews, Ian, Darrell and Kevin and bringing to the fore information that I would not otherwise have had. I also wish to thank Anne Bonney of Helm Press. Likewise 'The Bury and Radcliffe Times' for printing my letter requesting photographs and information and the many readers who contacted me, together with family and friends who have also been a great help.

The information contained is as accurate as possible so please excuse any slight error that I may have made along the way. The pictures are mostly my own, or friends or from people whom I have obtained permission to use.

I hope you enjoy my book I have tried to tell you a little of what life was like then for a 'townie' to be able to escape for weekends, school holidays, and Wakes Weeks, from the red bricks to the green slates of the Lake District. What life was like then, both at home in Radcliffe and country life, what it meant, the people and the freedom we enjoyed as children and then later the peace and beauty. Many of these memories I share with you are as clear as if they had happened yesterday! Please read on and enjoy!

Keith Holland
September 2005

Chapter One

Early Days

I was born into a family of twelve, six boys and six girls, the eleventh child and the youngest boy. There was just two years between our ages, which made it very easy when reckoning up how old everyone would be on his or her birthdays. Rene was the eldest, then Evelyn, then the two boys Sonny and Charles, followed by Madge and Ellis, Archie and Sybil, Audrey and Cecil, then me, Keith and Jean last of all. There was a gap of twenty-two years between the first and last. Although we lived in quite a large house, Rene and Sonny were married soon after I was born and Sybil sadly died when she was only five, before I was born. So the house was not overcrowded in that respect.

We lived at number 7 James Street, Radcliffe. It was a small town about seven miles north of Manchester. This was a large end terrace and we had a living room with sliding door (dad had put in) through to sitting room, kitchen, four bedrooms and bathroom upstairs. When we were small the bath could hold the four youngest. We had electricity. Radcliffe was a very busy town with varied industries, ranging from cotton, paper, iron, leather, coal and dozens of smaller industries, with a population in the 1920s of around twenty-five thousand people.

Charles Holland (dad)
in 1951

Charles Holland, my father, was a master painter and decorator and had started his business just a few years before the beginning of the First World War, so by the time I was born on the 9th August 1926 it was doing well. His father had been a bookkeeper and dad was one of six children and had served a decorating apprenticeship in Salford where he had lived with his elder brother Tom during this time. Both my grandfathers (on dad's side) lived in Stand Lane, the old Pilkington area of Radcliffe. Later when I was of school age I would see all the men dad employed setting off to go to their various jobs, some on their bikes, others pushing handcarts loaded with tackle and paints, whilst others going a little further afield were in dad's two American Chrysler cars. These would pull trailers and be driven by my two eldest brothers. They had their own sports cars and motorbikes that they used when they weren't working. Rene also had a motorcycle to knock about on before she was married.

Dad was a keen racing motorcyclist and was an amateur rider for Sunbeam Motorcycles and continued after I was born. He had won many cups and medals over the years and had lost the sight of his right eye in the process, although no one would ever have known. He never talked about it, it was as if the medals and cups weren't that important, only the thrill of racing and winning at the time.

Evelyn, my mother whose maiden name was Fraser, was one of eight children and had a very understanding and patient nature with us all. She was very friendly and kind, anyone coming to the door was welcomed into the kitchen for a cup of tea and a piece of cake, or freshly baked muffin. She was a wonderful cook. I can still savour the lovely cooking smells coming from the kitchen when Cecil and I raced home from school to scrape out the mixing bowls. The table would be full of pies and cakes, none of which lasted long and in the living room in front of the fire, there would always be two large baking bowls of rising dough. Mother was a very keen spiritualist; in fact we'd all been christened in the Spiritualist Church (Hall) – with flowers, which was the custom. Dad always said it was a load of bunkum, but as long as it made her happy he did not seem to mind.

Evelyn

Evelyn Holland (mother)
in 1951

I suppose in large families a few mix-ups can occur, like the time dad set off to register the birth of Cecil who should have been called Leslie. Dad decided to walk to the Council Offices but on the way stopped to talk to a plumber friend of his who just happened to be called Cecil. Everyone had been calling our Cecil, Leslie for nearly two years, until one day Rene who was working at the Council Offices, decided one lunch break to check through the family's birth certificates and discovered his name was down as Cecil, not Leslie! I don't think dad ever quite lived that one down!

In 1926 I was on the way, and mother had already decided my name was to be Keith Leslie should I be a boy. I'm not sure if dad was entrusted again to register either mine, or Jean's birth after the last mistake!

Another misunderstanding occurred again over names, apparently Sonny, our eldest brother's real name was Harry though this was never used and I was unaware of this. So it came as rather a surprise to me, when early on during the Second World War, a traveller for a paint company called to see if dad was at home but everyone was out except me. He asked how all my older brothers were doing in the Forces and in particular Harry. I said, 'I haven't got a brother called Harry!' He insisted and showed me the list of customers on his books i.e. - Harry and Charles Holland, who had started their own decorating business on the other side of town. I was astonished to say the least, at sixteen I didn't know I had a brother called Harry! Mother was first home and I told her what the traveller had said. Without hesitation she said, 'Oh yes, he's called Harry but your dad didn't like the name as it reminded him of someone he wasn't very keen on, so we always called him Sonny!'

We had another mistake or touch of forgetfulness, this time over birthdays. Soon after I started school the teacher said, 'Hands up who has a birthday next week?' I quickly put my hand up as my birthday was on the 4th but after checking on her list she said, 'No! Your birthday is on the 9th, the week after.' I said, 'It couldn't be as my mother had made me a birthday cake and told me it was on the 4th!' So it was another job for Rene at the Council Offices, who of course confirmed the teacher was right it was on the 9th, so I had two birthdays that year!

Town life in those days was a busy affair, with pedestrians, bicycles, buses and tramcars coming along the roads every few minutes. There were cars but more motorbikes with sidecars for those who could afford them. We had plenty of places of entertainment, with picture houses, dance halls and quite a large snooker hall that was underneath the Market Place, where the former world snooker champion, John Spencer used to practise. Every night I would see him carrying his snooker cue and case going to catch a bus to the 'Grotto' as it was known. During the war it was used as an air raid shelter.

Black Lane Bridge, Radcliffe early 1900s   Radcliffe Local History Society

Chapter Two

The Cottage

The first family holiday I remember was at the seaside at Cleveleys when we younger members of the family stayed at a boarding house with mother and two elder sisters. We had rather a disastrous time during our stay. First of all, Archie lost his new submarine. We were all paddling in the sea and he waded out a little further, winding it up and letting it go. It went under all right but never resurfaced! As you can imagine it was the end of the world for Archie and we never heard the last of it!

Jean, who was just a toddler at the time, wandered off through the open front door of the boarding house. She was nowhere to be found and there was a big search for her involving the police. Eventually a cleaning lady discovered her sitting on the front row of a theatre, waiting for the show to start! Stage life must have attracted her even at that early age, because by the time she was four she was actually performing her Shirley Temple (famous American child film star) routines on stage.

Our luck didn't change. Next, Cec was knocked down by a tramcar. They carried him into a chemist's shop, a doctor was called to examine him and fortunately he hadn't been badly hurt, to everyone's relief. I think the last straw came when Cec and I set the mattress on fire back at the boarding house. It had been raining that day and we had been playing under the bed using a lighted candle and completely forgot about it when we were called down to tea. I don't remember too much about it except that the landlady Mrs Crabtree was very cross with us, which she had every right to be.

We should have stayed for another week but Charlie arrived in dad's car to take us all back home at the end of that first ominous week! I'm sure mum and my elder sisters were very much relieved. Meanwhile at home things hadn't been going completely well without us. At work, dad had fallen into the lime-pot whilst slaking boiling lime. He had been standing on a plank, raking the cobbed lime to even it out, when the plank broke. Luckily he had managed to retain his balance to prevent himself falling in head first, but his legs were badly scalded before he managed to get out. So when we arrived home he was laying on the couch with both legs bandaged, but managed a smile when he saw us!

Early the following year (1930) when dad came in for tea one day he said he had been talking to Mr Charlton, one of his customers, about our

On the left Lound Cottage (taken from Bryan Beck), Woodside (Mr and Mrs Charlton's house) and Summer Hill (Mr Fred Cockerton) taken in 2005 (nothing has changed)

disastrous holiday in Cleveleys. He was a dentist who lived in Leyland but had his dental practise in Radcliffe. He said that he had a house in the Lake District where he and his wife spent their weekends and holidays and that there was a little cottage at the side of it that was unoccupied. He suggested to dad that if he got it, we could then use it to spend weekends and holidays in the countryside whenever we wanted. Mr Charlton went on to mention the fact that if on occasion we younger ones stayed over for the school holidays and were looked after by one of our elder sisters, this would obviously relieve the pressure on mother and those at home. This appeared a good idea all round. From all accounts Mr and Mrs Charlton were both looking forward to this proposition every bit as much as we were, as they didn't have any children of their own. So mother and father went with them the following weekend to view Lound Cottage. When they came back and told us what it was like, we couldn't wait to see it for ourselves but dad said, 'First, I'll make sure it was ours! It will need decorating and a few other things, but should be finished by Easter!'

This was going to be an exciting adventure for us all and particularly spending weeks in the countryside. First of all dad sent Sonny, Charlie and two of the workmen, Teddy, and Arnold, our cousin, for a week to decorate it throughout and paint the outside of Mr Charlton's house as well. They all stayed in Mr Charlton's house, Woodside, whilst the work was progressing. They completed all the work in double quick time so they could spend the rest of the week exploring the Lakes and enjoy the countryside and the different way of life. As Teddy put it, 'It was a very educational and enjoyable working holiday!'

The following weekend, the older members of the family made the trip to the cottage to clean and furnish it ready for Easter. Now it was ready for occupation, curtains, beds, carpets, table and chairs were in place and only needed the smaller items that we would bring with us when we came.

I shall always remember that first journey to the little cottage, there were no motorways in those days and although the traffic was nowhere near as heavy, there were narrow roads, bottlenecks and hold-ups to make the journey seem never ending. We travelled in dad's two big cars tucked in between pots, pans, sheets, towels and food, in fact 'everything bar the kitchen sink' but it was great fun and we were all excited. Dad stopped in Preston for toilets and to stretch our legs, before we set off again. He pointed out various places, names of towns and villages we were passing through. When we reached Lancaster, the castle looked impressive with its flags flying, the bustling market place where we all wandered around buying fresh food and various other items we needed for our two-week stay.

BOWLAND BRIDGE

John Marsh Collection

Early picture of Bowland Bridge

On the last lap of the journey, it was very noticeable to Audrey, Cec, Jean and myself, how different the colours and the landscape was becoming. We had all been used to red brick walls, drab grey slate rooftops, surrounded by tall mill chimneys belching out clouds of dirty smoke over the stone set streets. Now we appeared to be entering a fairyland of green fields and woods full of tall trees. There were cows, horses and sheep galore; white houses with greenstone and slate roofs, all so different from where we came from.

As we reached Milnthorpe dad said, 'Look over there, can you see the deer?' We all looked to the left to Dallam Park and saw the herd of fallow deer, the 'Bambi type' one associates with Walt Disney cartoons. It was the first time we had ever seen them in the wild, things were really getting exciting though we were beginning to wonder if we would ever reach the cottage. We continued along the new Princes Way to Levens Bridge, and dad told us, 'Only a few more miles now to go. Then just up the Lyth Valley to Bowland Bridge and it's only a country mile further.' At last! We would soon be at the cottage. When we reached Bowland Bridge, dad told us we would be able to walk down to the little shop here as they sold toffees, chocolate and pop. We went on up the steep hill and round the bend and dad pointed out the Strawberry Bank Inn where we could also call and get pop and crisps. We continued on the last half mile and as we approached the cottage we all had to close our eyes until he shouted, 'Right we're here! Open them!' There before us was our little cottage.

We all piled out of the car eager for our first look inside. How small it was compared to our home back in Radcliffe. I felt I could easily jump up and touch the ceilings. How quaint and inviting it was, with the refreshingly clean smell of the Walpamur water paint and the dark oak ceiling beams.

Aunt Clara with her grandson Ken Thornborrow in the 1930s

Chapter Three

Life in the Country

As soon as we had seen everything inside the cottage, which didn't take long, we all went outside to see what it was like. There was no back to it, just solid earth almost up to roof height and a raised garden to the left hand side of the cottage, with stone steps leading to an outside country toilet that was very primitive indeed (just a hole in the piece of wood where you sat with a bucket underneath). At the bottom of the stone steps on the cottage level was a woodshed where we could store all our odds and ends.

There was no electricity, just paraffin oil lamps and candles. There was a black iron range with a boiler on one side, with hooks to hang a kettle and pans for cooking. Later dad put a-small paraffin stove in the kitchen which was an addition but smelly. There was no running water, we had to get it all from a little well near the woodshed. It was all so different and exciting to us!

Dad sent us to Bryan Beck Farm which was only a hundred yards away round the corner to get milk, eggs and butter, that had already been ordered, and they would get tea ready. The four of us walked into the farmyard and Mr and Mrs Thornborrow obviously knew we were coming and knew all our names. Uncle Fred and his wife Aunt Clara (as we were to call them afterwards) had three daughters but two were married and lived away. The youngest one, Cathy, was the same age as Madge our elder sister, around seventeen at the time so they hit it off straight away and became good friends. They invited us to come round whenever we wanted to.

Aunt Clara showed us into the dairy where she had the milk churn; we were all fascinated with it; a large wooden barrel on a stand with highly polished brass fittings and a glass window that you could look through and see the milk thickening up as the handle was turned. Cec and I would often help Aunt Clara to churn the milk, as we got older. The dairy was always very clean and cool in a room at the back of the farmhouse, with polished flag floors and working surfaces where the hen and duck eggs, butter and cheese were kept. Before this we had only seen them in shops but now we were actually seeing where they came from and how the butter and cheese were made. Aunt Clara showed us how she patted the butter into shape with the wooden paddles (or butter pats).

We made our way back to the cottage and excitedly told everybody what we had seen. Tea was ready for us, there wasn't enough room round the table for everyone but it was all right as the elder ones were busy anyway, making up beds and seeing to other chores. We hurried our teas down in order to get back to the farm again as quickly as we could, Cec and myself to see Uncle Fred milking the cows and Audrey and Jean to help with feeding the calves and chickens.

Cec and I made our way to the shippon where we could hear Uncle Fred getting cross with a cow that kept swishing its tail round his head and wouldn't stand still while he was milking her. When he saw us at the door, he shouted for us to come in but it was a rather narrow passageway between the backs of the cows and the other end of the shippon. We were a bit scared in case they kicked out but finally after a bit of coaxing, Cec took my hand and we crept slowly along. When we got nearer Uncle Fred, he said, 'Have you ever tasted warm milk straight from the cow, instead of cold right out of a bottle?' We both said, 'No!' And with that he quickly swivelled round on his stool and squirted milk in our faces. I think he'd been longing to do that for years, as he didn't have any boys in his own family to tease. With a big grin on his face he just said, 'You forgot to open your mouths!' He loved to play pranks on us as we found out over the following months and that was one of the things he did.

Meanwhile, Audrey and Jean were having a good time acquainting themselves with the rest of the animals on the farm when we joined them. They brought us in mind of our own farmyard animals we'd got for Christmas, but these were real and much more interesting. They had everything, horses, cows, pigs and sheep. There were hens, ducks, geese and turkeys wandering about the farmyard and there was always a lovely smell of burning wood about the place, as it wafted down from the chimney pots. This was just like another world, and we all loved it.

The day had been a long and busy one, so we younger ones weren't too late going to bed whilst our elder brothers and sisters walked down to the Hare and Hounds, in Bowland Bridge for the evening, and mother and dad sat in below quietly talking. We only had two bedrooms, but three double beds, mother and dad in one bedroom whilst the elder sisters occupied one of the double beds in our room. We were all tucked up in the other double bed but sideways on, not lengthways. The elder brothers had to sleep downstairs on the floor that night.

I remember us all lying there by the light of a candle whilst Archie made us feel all creepy telling his ghost stories, which was made even more chilling with the owl hoots coming from the woods behind the cottage, then an odd high pitched scream in the distance which Archie said would be a werewolf. Probably a stoat with a rabbit, but we weren't to know then, all the country noises.

In spite of his efforts to scare us all to death we all went soundly to sleep, only to be wakened up sharply, around midnight with a very loud crashing noise followed by much laughter, and scuffling around. Wondering what the commotion was all about we all got up to find out what it was. Then when we looked in mother and dad's room we could see that the leg of the bed had gone through the floor and mother was still on the floor in her nightdress whilst everyone was having a good laugh. It had been the end of a very exhausting day for them and mother had just flopped on the bed tired out, anyway the boys moved the bed and we all went to sleep again. There was a patch on the kitchen ceiling for a few years after, a timely reminder of that very first day we had spent in the Lake District.

Bryan Beck Farm – nothing has changed since the 1930s

Next morning most of us wakened early with the sound of a cock crowing. It was strange at first wondering where we were and then everything dawned on us. Cec and I were up with the larks! We had promised to help Uncle Fred with the cows. We quickly dressed, had a drink of milk, a hunk of jam and bread, then slipped out of the door leaving everyone dozing!

Uncle Fred let us feed the cows with some 'cow cakes' (as he called them) that they chewed when being milked. In later years with the help of Midge the sheepdog we used to sometimes take the cows back to the nearby fields to graze. Uncle Fred seemed to enjoy our company, as we did his and all his amusing tales. After milking we went back to the cottage for breakfast. The elder ones had already had theirs and the table was set for us young ones. We had almost finished when Mrs Charlton appeared at the door. She said excitedly, 'Oh children, what a lovely surprise! The wood fairies must have known you were coming and they've left you presents in the orchard.' We just looked at one another with mouths open. She didn't wait for a reply and went on to say, 'When you have finished your breakfast, come quickly. They are probably waiting in the wood to see you open them!'

I'm not sure whether we believed in fairies or not but we nevertheless followed her into the orchard and there sure enough hanging on the branches of the trees were four little presents with our names on. They were each carefully wrapped containing chocolates and sweets. It had certainly been a lovely surprise. So who could not believe in fairies after that?

Afterwards, mum and dad took us to Windermere, over Gummers Howe where we stopped to see the steamers sailing on the lake, and then to Bowness and Ambleside, so that we saw the whole length of it. Dad said he would take us all the way round next time but we had to get back for lunch as Uncle Fred was going to take us a walk over his top fields.

Mum and dad obviously wanted to get us acquainted and interested in our new surroundings so that we would want to stay at the cottage with Madge without having to be coaxed. Cec and I wouldn't need any coaxing, it was an instant hit with us all, especially with all the attractions on the farm that Audrey and Jean also found new and exciting.

After lunch, everyone set off from the farmhouse up the little lane leading to the top fields along the Gummers Howe range. Uncle Fred was pointing out where his land was as we walked along the cart track. Then he pointed his stick towards a stream on the right hand side of the track wending its way down towards the farm, 'That's our water supply and yours as well,' he said. 'Crystal clear and never dries up. In fact the farm was named after the stream, Bryan Beck.' Uncle Fred turned to us younger boys and said, 'There's plenty of trout in yon beck you can tickle.' Everyone burst out laughing when Jean said in her young inquisitive voice, 'Why, does it make them laugh?' Never having heard the expression before, this was a typical question from one so young. I was only two years older and wasn't exactly sure what the joke was, but Cec and I would find out in the next two weeks.

As we wound our way up the track past the lower meadows and fields we eventually went through a gate onto more open ground and we were looking back down into the Winster valley which was quite breathtaking. As young as we were, it was a view we'd have imprinted on our minds for ever, the hills in the distance, the trees and patchwork of fields in the valley below, with wild daffodils sprouting all over, it was something one had to see for oneself to realise its full beauty.

A little further along Uncle Fred turned round, and then held his finger to his lips for us to be quiet. Then pointing to a stone wall a little further ahead, we walked silently towards it. Over the other side was a long flat meadow and over the other side of that, another wall, then beyond that, nothing but woodland rising to the very top of the Gummers Howe range. Charlie lifted me up to peep over the wall, and there in the centre of the field was a small heard of red deer. There was about a dozen altogether, much bigger than the ones we'd seen the day before on our journey to the cottage, but after we'd been watching them for a minute or two, they must have sensed us and looked our way. Then, in an instant they were over the wall, disappearing into the dense woodland beyond. It was time to be turning back now, Uncle Fred would have to milk, and the elder members of the family would have to get ready to return to Radcliffe. So we made our way back on a slightly different route, through small woodland, where the beck flowed through. We saw about six or seven more deer but this time they were much smaller than the red ones we had been watching. Uncle Fred told us they were roe deer. I think we had just about seen everything that day, rabbits galore, scurrying around pheasants. Hawks and many other types of birds Uncle Fred had pointed out to us.

Audrey, Cec, Jean and me could not believe all this was happening to us, such an adventure, we'd never seen anything like this before, all the family was enjoying every minute of it too, how different it all was from home, so

Cec, myself (Keith), Jean and Audrey sitting on the wall facing Lound Cottage in the 1930s

clean and green. The fresh air and the openness made a big impression on us all. Us four would be staying for two whole weeks with Madge, mother and dad were also staying on for a few more days but Evelyn would be going back with Sonny, Charlie, Ellis and Archie, to look after them when they came home from work. Ellis had just started work in dad's business, along with the eldest two, but Archie who was still on holiday from school returned to be with Ellis. Cec and me were both a little too young for his type of activity but whilst we were all walking back after our long uphill walk, us younger ones were glad we had elder brothers to give us piggy backs as we were not used to all this hill walking.

After tea, Evelyn and our older brothers set off for Radcliffe. They would have a more peaceful time with us not being there and could now take it in turns to have their holidays in the cottage. Everyone in the family was completely satisfied with the way things were working out. Even Mr and Mrs Charlton next door had found a new interest in their lives, the girls would keep her company and later dad would bring Mr Charlton along fishing with us during the following summer holidays. So it really had been a very good proposition.

For the next few days dad would take us round the lakes. I remember he would sit Cec and me in turn on his knee and let us pretend we were driving, but only of course on private stretches of road where there was no other traffic. The car had a long front bench seat in leather with a pull down armrest that Jean liked to sit on between mum and dad. Each day we would set off for different places with a picnic basket, Grange-over-Sands with its lovely large open air swimming pool, (we would visit this often in the summer months) then other days, Hawkshead, Keswick, Ullswater and a steamer trip on the lake. Dad put us on the steamer with mother and Madge at the Lakeside landings, Newby Bridge and picked us up when we arrived in Bowness.

Thursday evening arrived and mum and dad returned to Radcliffe and the business, leaving Madge to look after us, returning on the Saturday afternoon for the weekend. I think this was a trial period for us to see how we would react without them, but they needn't have worried one little bit, as there was far too much to occupy our minds. Madge was just like another mother to us and of course she had Cathy from the farm if she needed any help or advice with matters concerning our new surroundings. Also we had Mr and Mrs Charlton just next-door and they very helpful, so it wasn't really as if we were completely on our own.

Soon after tea mum and dad set off, taking us down to Bowland Bridge with them in the car. Then after making sure we had enough sweets, they set off on their long drive back. Madge had strict orders to contact them everyday from the public phone box in Bowland Bridge, to tell them how we were getting on.

It was a long walk back, mostly uphill but we took our time, as there was nothing to hurry for, there was no television those days. By the time we reached our little cottage I think we were all ready for supper and bed. It had been a very busy time for everyone and by now we were all used to hearing the owls in the wood at the back and the rustling of the trees around us, it had already become part of our new life, we never needed rocking to sleep!

Although the cottage was on the side of a lane, traffic in those days was almost non-existent, except for the few vans that came around supplying food and other household requirements. Every Monday and Friday the butcher – Simpson's from Underbarrow. We had Kit Simpson in the 1930s, then his nephew Harry took over and he had a little shop in Underbarrow. Tuesday and Friday the grocer's van – Hughes from Windermere. Wednesday the fresh fish van from Flookburgh about eleven miles away. They were so fresh it was possible to see their tails and fins moving slightly. It was an open van with various types of fish displayed in boxes along either side. Cec and I would eagerly try to pick these out and get Madge to buy them for dinner. On Thursdays, Clarks the ironmonger's van from Windermere would arrive, selling candles, paraffin, wicks, dolly blue, soap, shovels, brushes, in fact anything one needed for the household. So who needed fridges or freezers then! Just a cool pantry was ideal, and the eggs, milk and butter we got fresh from the farm.

Madge and Cathy Thornborrow
in the 1930s

Denise Beck (Madge's daughter)

Beatrice (Charlie's wife) on the left and Kathleen (Sonny's wife)
on motorbikes in Sion Street, Radcliffe

Denise Beck

Chapter Four

Tickling Trout

The following morning after breakfast Cec and I decided to see if we could catch any of these fish in the beck that Uncle Fred had told us about. He said that we didn't need any fishing tackle, the best way was to feel under the stones with our hands and then when we had our hand round the fish, we had to throw it onto the bank.

We tried this method for quite a long time but without success, as they always seemed to get away. As we worked our way a little further upstream Cec felt under a rock and whispered, 'I've got one!' At the same time he managed to quickly throw it onto the side, I got out of the water and put it in a bucket. I think we must have had visions of filling the bucket but we were eager to get back and show it to Uncle Fred and besides my feet were getting cold. We decided to go back and have it for dinner. Uncle Fred had a big smile on his face when we showed it to him. He said it would be very tasty when fried in butter, but when we got back to the cottage, Madge wouldn't do it for us, so disappointedly we had to throw it back in the beck.

They say practise makes perfect and we certainly put plenty of practise in during the next few days, although I just didn't seem to have Cec's knack. I couldn't believe it when I actually caught one but for each one I managed to catch Cec would always catch three or four. The cold water didn't seem to affect him like me, so I always preferred to stay on the side and put them in the bucket when he threw them out.

This was all very interesting and exciting stuff, Madge didn't mind at all, it was keeping us occupied every morning whilst she was doing the household chores and preparing our lunch. Audrey and Jean would either be at the farm or at Mrs Charlton's next door. So everyone was happy. This was a little different from our holidays in Cleveleys. After tea Mr Charlton took Madge and the girls down to the telephone box in Bowland Bridge to phone mum and dad, then brought them back again in his car. Cec and I would be busy at the farm with Uncle Fred or in the beck, which we'd got quite addicted to.

On Saturday afternoon we all walked down to Bowland Bridge to meet mum and dad coming up to the cottage for the weekend. This time we wouldn't have to walk all the way back up the hill, Jean was only two years old so this would save us pushing her back in her pushchair when her legs got tired. While waiting for the car to appear we would entertain ourselves on the bridge, playing boat races, throwing twigs into the water, then running to the other side to see whose appeared first. Then when dad's car appeared in the village we all ran to greet them with smiling faces. Cec and I couldn't wait to tell dad about the fish we'd caught in the beck with our bare hands and everything else that had happened. It must have been a relief to them to see us so happy and settled, which meant there would be no tears or sullen faces when they came to leave us on the Sunday, as we all knew they would be coming back again the week after.

We had a pleasant weekend and it was time for them to go and we all travelled along the road in the car as far as the next farm, Addyfield about a quarter of a mile further along the road, then we got out and waved goodbye from there. We could see dad's car disappearing down the hill and waited for it to reappear as it was going along past the village in the valley below. We were still waving from that distance, whether they could see us or not, but then it was gone and we walked back, just a little sad that they had left us but Madge had us all singing, to take our minds off their departure.

Our second week came and passed with Cec and me exploring further up the beck each day, we were both by now getting a little more expert in catching the trout. Dad had bought us a pair of black wader type Wellingtons, I found them very useful but Cec always seemed to prefer being in the beck in his bare feet.

When Cec caught his first eel, he had been feeling under a rock, when he suddenly shouted, 'A fish has bitten me!' He put his finger to his mouth. Undaunted, he was determined to catch it, which he did, flinging it out onto the bank wriggling and squirming away. It was an eel, the first we had seen let alone caught. We were both quite excited it was so slippery we could hardly hold it. We couldn't put it into the bucket with the trout we'd caught, as we were frightened it might eat them. So we had to put it back in the water.

Feeling quite pleased with our catch we carried the bucket containing the four or five trout back with us just in time to see the fish van from Flookburgh in the farmyard. We had met the fish man the week before when both Aunt Clara and mother had bought some fish. We told him that we were keen on fishing and he said he would show us how to clean them ready for cooking. I think we were both a little worried about this, catching them was one thing but killing them was different. He tried to help us by saying that if we hadn't caught them, eels, herons or kingfishers possibly would have.

This time Madge did cook them for us and as Uncle Fred had said, they were indeed very tasty. He also told us how to clean and cook eels and went on tell us how they fed on smaller fish, so we now made a point of catching

Leslie Butler delivering fish on a Wednesday to Mrs Shackleton
at Little Hartbarrow Farm just after the war   Jack Manning

them. Cec even devised a way of catching them more easily by dangling a
worm on a hook in front of the stone then when its head popped out, he
would grab it with a pair of Madge's curling tongs. This worked a treat, we
were learning fast every day!

By the end of the second week, living in the cottage had become second
nature to us. Cec and I would take turns fetching water from the well, and
wood and coal for the fire. Audrey and Jean would bring fresh milk and eggs
from the farm whilst Madge would see to all our meals, and generally, look
after us very well.

When mum and dad arrived again on the Saturday afternoon, we met them
as before in the village with the same enthusiasm as the previous week, so,
the experiment had worked out very well for everyone. Madge had made a
new friend in Cathy, Mr and Mrs Charlton's lives had been made a little
more fuller. We young ones had found a happier and more interesting way
to spend our days and mum and dad now had more time to themselves,
even if only during the holiday periods.

We knew we would be going home again the next day because Audrey and Cec would be starting school on the following Monday. I would be starting school in September but that was a long time off and we would be coming back to the cottage for other holidays before then. It had been a lovely two weeks.

It was time to go back home and leave this wonderful green world of fields and trees, animals, wild birds, and our little cottage, so we said goodbye to Uncle Fred and Aunt Clara at the farm and Mr and Mrs Charlton and started on our long journey home, but not quite as cramped up as we had been two weeks before. I think we must have all quietened down probably realising that we wouldn't be able to get up in a morning and listen to the farmyard sounds and country noises, or the smell of burning wood. All these things we would miss, instead smoky coal chimneys would replace them, and the sound of dozens of clogs clattering on the pavement as the mill girls hurried along to work. I don't remember too much after Preston. I suppose we must have all dropped off to sleep. It had been the end of a perfect holiday, but it certainly wouldn't be the last.

Now the elder end of the family would make good use of the little cottage for their holidays and odd weekends whenever we younger ones stayed at home in the red brick environment. They loved the cottage in the Lake District just as we did, it was something for them to look forward to whenever we weren't in residence.

Back in Radcliffe things went on as before, the next holiday we would be looking forward to would be at Whitsun, a long way off, as far as we were concerned. When it did arrive, I remember all the processions in the town; schools of children parading through the main streets displaying their banners and people throwing pennies and halfpennies in their path as they walked along. It gave many parents and relations a great feeling of pride to see their children dressed in their finery, walking along with their different schools accompanied by their teachers. Whit Friday was a special day for many towns in those days, bringing out a great feeling of togetherness and enjoyment in the community.

I remember too the 'heavy industry' processions, as they passed through the streets displaying their products on gaily painted carts pulled by teams of powerful horses groomed to perfection, with highly polished leather harnesses, decorated with shiny horse brasses, black leaded hooves and coloured plumes waving above their head. We would see these horses every day pulling long heavy carts past our house from the paper mill at the end of our street loaded with very large heavy reels of paper, but to see them like this in all their glory was a sight to remember.

Sadly most of the town's industry has now gone, never to return, even the paper mill at the end of the street is no longer there but the memory of those childhood days will always be there, I just close my eyes and listen to those powerful horses snorting and straining away, pulling their heavy loads up to the paper mill over the stone set streets.

I remember a cobbler who had a little shop in Radcliffe, he was called Jimmy, his shop was close by, so we as young boys would congregate in his shop to help him with errands or other little jobs he couldn't quite manage himself. Jimmy's legs had been blown off in the First World War but a more jovial person one couldn't wish to meet.

He would sit there on his stool, cutting and shaping leather, or making clogs for the mill girls, and the miners who worked down the pit. We would help him to make studs out of the bits of scrap leather for our football boots; the enjoyment of each other's company was mutual. Jimmy never complained about his misfortune and never talked about the war that had deprived him of his legs, in fact I remember him saying to one new lad who had started to come into the shop. 'Before you can join our club you'll have to see if you can make me shout, 'Stop!' Then he invited him to kick his shins underneath the counter opening where the top lifted up – kick me as hard as you can he said or I won't feel it, we all kept our faces straight as the young lad kicked as hard as he could but of course it hurt him more than Jimmy who's legs were made of tin.

On another occasion he would send them on an errand to a shop on the other side of town with a request for the glass hammer and rubber nails he'd lent them a couple of weeks before, of course they knew of Jimmy's pranks and would send them to another shop, saying they'd borrowed them. Finally the lad would come back 'fagged out' saying, 'they're still using them Jimmy!' Then Jimmy would give him a bag of sweets and a leather badge with 'Jimmy's Club' stamped on it.

I was looking forward to Saturday for we would be setting off on our second holiday to the little cottage and this time we all knew what to expect

The Lyth Valley – damsons in blossom (Hotel on right)   John Marsh Collection

Rene with her husband Joe Davenport outside the cottage in 1932

Chapter Five

Country Ways

The journey this time didn't seem quite as long, but then we weren't packed in like sardines, as before. Our first stop would be at a level crossing at Houghton where more often than not the gates would be closed for quite a while to let the train through. Nobody minded the wait, as dad would nip out and buy everyone a large ice cream cornet from a wooden hut conveniently situated at the roadside. Once through, we would be on our way towards Preston, then past George Formby's (popular music hall type singer with banjo ukulele in 1930-40s) house and on to Lancaster, where we would always stop to wander around the open-air market, then again on the last lap to the green fields beyond.

The excitement of seeing the cottage again and the thought of staying for another week, had been building up in our minds since Easter, and we could hardly wait to get there. When we finally arrived everywhere seemed greener than ever and this time we all knew exactly what we were going to do after looking round the cottage.

Uncle Fred must have been waiting for us to arrive, and knew we would be appearing in the farmyard. Cec and I ran straight from the cottage with Audrey and Jean straggling a little behind, which was probably just as well, for as soon as we both ran through the open gate into the yard a headless chicken came flying out of the woodshed, followed by its head. It's body ran round in circles with wings flapping a couple of times, then dropped, whilst its eyes blinked a few times before finally shutting. We stood with our mouths wide open wondering what had happened. Then we saw Uncle Fred peeping out of the woodshed grinning. Suddenly Aunt Clara appeared at the farmhouse door and shouted over to him, 'Fancy doing a thing like that! They're only townies, they don't understand country ways yet!' Then proceeded to give him the length of her tongue.

Seeing the hen had not really frightened us, just the initial surprise of watching it circling round without its head and when Audrey and Jean arrived a few minutes later it was just lying dead. Uncle Fred simply said, 'They have to be killed before you can 'cook em' and that's the quickest way to do it - they know now't about it!' Maybe we were townies but we were learning fast.

Our second holiday went quickly doing much the same as before but this time we brought one or two board games with us to play when it rained.

We had a wireless set (radio) so we could keep in touch with the outside world, though the sound used to fade and crackle as if it was coming from outer space and was powered by an accumulator (sometimes called a wet battery). This had to be regularly charged and we took this to Johnny Gilpin (an invalid) that lived in the next cottage (Hartbarrow) about quarter of a mile away and would be exchanged for a fully charged one that cost 6d (2p) that had already been charged by his generator. His father was killed in the First World War and he lived with his mother and earned his living repairing items for local people from his little shed in the garden.

Even tramps in those days had pride and respect for people, as I well remember the time Cec and I walked into Uncle Fred's farmyard to see an old tramp with long grey hair and a beard, coming out of the farmhouse door with a brown paper parcel under his arm. We both froze, not knowing what to do but he just touched his hat, then tied the parcel onto an old bicycle that was absolutely laden down with an array of pans and bundles containing all his worldly goods. When he'd finished tying the parcel on he turned round, touched his hat again, then went on his way pushing the bicycle, there was no way he could ride it, when he'd gone we went into the farmhouse but Aunt Clara wasn't in, the place was empty. So we ran up to the fields where everyone was busy 'scaling the hay!' (Scattering thinly).

We told Uncle Fred that we'd seen this funny old man coming out of the door with a parcel tucked under his arm but he just drawled, 'Oh! That's only Lancashire Bill, he always comes around this time ert year!' 'But what about the parcel he had?' we said. 'Oh, just an auld pair of boots and socks. We always leave him a meal on table and he always chops us a pile of kindling wood in return,' said Uncle Fred casually.

Seldom doors would be locked. Back home, our own back door was always left open in those days but we were never burgled. We often saw Lancashire Bill each year around the same time, just as Uncle Fred had mentioned, he always gave a polite nod and a murmur as he went on his never ending travels, pushing his bike along the winding lanes to who knows where.

Whenever we approached the Lyth Valley Hotel in the 1930s dad would turn around to we young ones sitting in the back of the car and say with a little smile on his face, 'Who wants to walk to the cottage from here?' Then we would look at each other and force a grin. It's only another four or five miles he would add. Dad was having his little joke of course, because one hot Saturday in the summer of 1931 when I was five, we'd set off to meet mother and dad who would be coming up to the cottage for the weekend. Madge our sister had given us all our lunches and two pence each to spend then waved us off on our way to Bowland Bridge. When we got there we bought pop and sweets, then waited for the car to appear, playing boat races on the bridge as usual.

Then as time passed, we decided to walk on further, still no car, and then further still! They surely must be coming any minute now? But still no car, what could have happened? We could turn back but we were hot and getting tired, our pop had run out too, what should we do? We'd already come further than we'd intended and time was getting on, going back past Bowland would mean climbing Smithy Hill up to Strawberry Bank, then more hills to the cottage. So on and on we went, we knew this was the way dad had always come and even if he'd decided to come a different way, when he'd reached the cottage, he would have come straight away to look for us. By now we were approaching the Lyth Valley Hotel, maybe they would let us have a drink of something until dad and mother arrived, we'd often called there for refreshments so the man would recognise us surely. Cec, Audrey and myself were taking turns carrying Jean, who was only three on our backs, when at last the hotel came into view. What a glorious sight it was, just as though we had crossed the desert, but still so sign of the car. In fact, I think we'd only met two horses and carts leading hay from the fields in all that time.

We all flopped down quite exhausted with the ordeal, wishing we'd stayed at home with Madge, who would be worried to death wondering what had happened to us. Cec and I decided to knock on the front door and ask for a drink, we'd spent all our money in Bowland, even a drink of water would be more than welcome.

Just as we were about to knock Audrey shouted excitedly, 'A car! A car!' There in the distance we could see a car coming along the road. Both Cec and I could tell it was dad's car even from that distance, so we ran back to Audrey and Jean excitedly. At last, they were here, just when we'd given them up. We all stood up waving our hands as the car approached, but it sailed on through without stopping. We couldn't see mother in the front seat and dad was looking the other way. We stood there for a second or two unbelievingly, then Cec and I started to run after him waving and shouting, but then it disappeared round the bed and was gone. We both turned round and started to walk back to the girls in despair but when we got to them dad had turned around and was coming back, he was having us on, pretending he hadn't seen us.

It seemed that dad had taken mother into Manchester to stay with one of her sisters who had been taken ill, which was why he was later than usual, but at least he'd arrived and as the saying goes, 'better late than never!'

Low Ludderburn (recent photograph) one time home of Arthur Ransome.
Left the building he used as his study and house just out of sight on right.

Early postcard of the Hare and Hounds, Bowland Bridge   John Marsh Collection

Madge was in the telephone box at Bowland Bridge, having borrowed Cathy's bike she'd been phoning Radcliffe trying to find out what had happened when dad hadn't arrived and we couldn't be found either. When we eventually got back to the cottage the tea table was set and we were once again feeling happy. I don't think we needed much rocking to sleep that night!

This was the way we would spend all our holidays in the 1930s and each time there would be a new adventure to experience. Dad had by now managed to find a place at the side of Lake Windermere, where we could spend a day relaxing by the shore, or fishing in the rowing boat dad had bought. We boys would make good use of it. Now we were able to fish for pike, perch and trout with fishing rods, which gave both Cec and me a further interest into our newly found sport, we would spend many happy Sundays over the next few years doing just this.

Often we would take Mr Charlton along, he was beginning to enjoy his outings on the lake fishing and whenever we boys caught a fish and couldn't get the hook out, he was there to help with his de-hooking gadgets. He had acquired all the fishing tackle especially for these outings and was so methodical with everything he did; to watch him extracting a hook was like watching him in his surgery taking out a tooth, so gentle and caring. I knew this because later he took an aching tooth out for me back at the cottage and I didn't feel a thing, so I knew the fish wouldn't either, such a kindly gentle man who always reminded me of an elderly Charlie Chaplin (comedian from the early 1920s black and white silent movies), with white hair.

Low Ludderburn was the next cottage on our way to the lake, this was about a mile away and although we didn't know it then, it was where Arthur Ransome lived, the author of 'Swallows and Amazons'. He would always nod and smile in neighbourly acknowledgement. Mr Charlton told us about the time his old dog-called Banter, which was blind, had wandered across in front of Mr Ransome's car. He stopped and had quite a long chat to Mr Charlton before driving away.

Dad would always take us rides in the car each weekend when he and mother came up to the cottage during holiday times. I remember once when we went to visit some of mum and dad's friends, who had stayed at our cottage and liked the countryside here so much that they bought their own cottage near Witherslack, and one day we travelled through Witherslack woods to visit them. As we came to the edge of the wood there was a small cottage on the roadside. Dad said, 'You see that cottage? Well, that's the cottage where Little Red Riding Hood's Grandma lived and this is the wood where Red Riding Hood came through to visit her. So keep your eyes open for any wolves as we go through!'

Little Cottage (North Lodge) before you go through Witherslack Woods

Early postcard showing Witherslack Hall

John Marsh Collection

The wood was very dark and dense, the road very winding, as we slowly wound our way through with us young ones in the back peering out of the car windows with eyes wide open looking for wolves. Suddenly dad stopped the car quickly and said, 'Look! A wolf! Did you see it?' All our eyes looked in the direction where he was pointing and sure enough a brown object was moving through the trees, then disappeared. It was probably a deer, but we were all convinced it was a wolf. Then as we carried on along the road it was easy to imagine the woodman with his axe and Little Red Riding Hood skipping along the road with her basket.

As we finally came out of the wood dad pointed to a big house on the left and said, 'That's Witherslack Hall, where Little Red Riding Hood lived with her father, Lord Stanley.' Dad must have been having a quite chuckle to himself and mum just went along with it. Later, of course we all realised it was just dad's way of keeping us interested as we rode along and of course we were at the right age to let our imagination do the rest.

It was bluebell time in the woods, probably the best time of the year to drive or walk through. I always make a point of driving through the fairy tale wood each year at this time, just to remind me of the first time we went through, I used to tell my own children and grandchildren the same story when they were young too, but I don't think quite as convincingly as dad did. The wood has been thinned down now to what it was then, many of the taller trees have been felled and the bluebells do not seem quite as prolific but the cottage is still there, and Witherslack Hall (although now a school) but the memory of that first car ride through will always remain!

Once past Lord Stanley's residence, we would cut off the road along a narrow lane, the fields there would be teeming with rabbits, far too many to try and count, but this was long before myxomatosis was introduced. Cec and I would simply look to see how many black ones we could see.

Then when we arrived at Beckhead where Mr and Mrs Warburton's cottage was situated, Audrey and Jean would play with their two younger daughters. One of their elder sisters, Lily ran a dancing school for children back in Radcliffe over her fathers shop, so it was inevitable that Audrey and Jean would be joining the dancing troupe in the coming winter months.

Mr Warburton had a car exactly like dad's, even down to the same colours, blue/grey with black mudguards, it was difficult to tell them apart and I remember many Sunday evenings when returning back home to Radcliffe, we would meet at their cottage then change cars. We would travel home in their car with Madge and Dorothy, one of their elder daughters, driving, whilst mum and dad, Mr and Mrs Warburton would be able to enjoy peace and quiet without interruption from we young ones on the way home. This suited everyone, as Dorothy was an excellent driver and even entertained us with ghost stories and songs on the journey.

Dorothy came over from Witherslack one day in her father's car and suggested that we go down to the lake for the day with it being so hot, so we all jumped in the back of the car loaded with picnic baskets, costumes and the Li-Lo (airbed), we hadn't got the little wooden chalet just then.

When we arrived at Blakeholme Bay costumes were donned and the Li-Lo inflated for a good play about on the water, but we found it a little too stony for comfort on our feet, so we explored a little further along and discovered the perfect place to paddle. We showed this to Madge and Dorothy who said it would be perfectly safe to play there but when they shouted us for drinks or lunch we had to run right back and not wander off anywhere, which we didn't. It was very well sheltered, a small and shallow lagoon like inlet, around to the left of the opening between the island and the shoreline. The bottom was soft with silt and warm with the sunshine beating down on it. We couldn't have found a better place. Madge had rubbed us all with sun cream and we had responded whenever they had shouted us, so the day was spent just enjoying ourselves, playing about in the water and running backwards and forwards for drinks etc. But now it was time to go, Madge and Dorothy had just shouted for us to return, but instead of returning along the shoreline as we were supposed to do, we decided to paddle back on the Li-Lo, which meant passing through the narrow strip of water separating the island on the right from the mainland.

When the water was low during dry weather spells it was easy to walk through the shallow water to the island but when the water was high rowing boats could easily pass through. We couldn't paddle through it, as the water was very low indeed, so we all got off except Jean, pulling it through with her on it. Once through we all jumped on it again and started to paddle away towards Madge and Dorothy, who were now dressed and preparing to leave.

We had just managed to go a short distance on the water, when both Cec and myself noticed the Li-Lo was beginning to submerge a little, so we slid off and started to push and pull it towards the shore. Both Cec and I could swim, we knew that Jean couldn't and Audrey the eldest could, providing she had one foot on the bottom but then they noticed it was sinking too and the air was filled with screams and shouts for 'Help!' Madge and Dorothy ran down to the waters edge, saw what was happening and shouted to us to 'hang on!' Dorothy was stripping down to her underwear, and then

36

Sister Madge in the boat at Blakeholme with the little island behind in the 1930s   Denise Beck

quickly dived in, whilst Madge was running over to a rowing boat further around the bay. No one else was about, except for the man who owned it; he also had heard the girls' cries and was running towards it too.

In the meantime Cec and myself were trying to keep the Li-Lo afloat with Jean still on it, whilst Audrey was hanging on for grim death but had the presence of mind to doggie paddle with her legs. Dorothy was streaking towards us like 'Tarzan's Jane' and managed to reach us before the situation got even worse. Another minute or two and the consequences could have been much greater. A few minutes later, the rowing boat arrived with Madge and the owner, Jean and Audrey were pulled into the boat to everyone's relief, whilst we hung on behind and were towed back, with the deflated Li-Lo. It had been a narrow escape, one that we would never forget in a hurry and in fact even now we all have vivid memories of that almost disastrous day.

It seemed that when we'd pulled the Li-Lo through the gap with Jean still on it, it must have caught on a sharp stone and received a slow puncture but I suppose none of this would have happened had we not disobeyed Madge's instructions.
The long summer holidays came and went, spending many happy hours in the fields haymaking. Uncle Fred would show us how to rake, or stack the hay in the barn, and then Cec and I would ride back to the fields in the cart.

It was all very exciting and great fun. Cathy and Madge would help Aunt Clara with 'the drinkin' (picnic) when it was time for a break.

The sweet smell of the hay was out of this world, we would lie there at the end of the day with our eyes closed listening to the twittering of the birds, the sound of buzzing bees and distant bird calls. Then open our eyes to see the swallows swooping in the sky – truly wonderful!

Our journeys down to the village shop for sweets now became more interesting, looking for wild strawberries at the roadside or bilberries. Cec and me had discovered a pear tree in the middle of a field and we would dare each other to raid it but the pears were a little hard and we decided to leave them until they properly ripened. Unfortunately when we tried again on another occasion, Audrey shouted to us that there was a bull in the field so we quickly made our exit back over the wall! We were due back home and school again, we never did get to try those pears!

Chapter Six

Jelly Making and Grandma's Bloomers

The school holidays were made up of two weeks at Easter, three weeks July and August, back to school and off for two weeks in September, these were called Wakes Weeks. This was when traditionally the mill workers had their holidays and the mills simply closed down. Different towns would take different weeks to ease congestion at seaside resorts. Whole families would catch the trains to Blackpool, Southport and other popular resorts for a week by the sea at a boarding house, take in the sea air, Punch and Judy and various shows. Not as many people went to the Lakes then.

Our September holidays arrived and we looked forward again to our time at the cottage. This now had become so much a part of our lives. Cec and I spent much of our time fishing in the beck and helping Uncle Fred on the farm. We also went walks round about or down to the village. Then when mum and dad came up each Saturday afternoon we would picnic by the lakeside or take the rowing boat out for a spot of fishing. One day we were driving past Bowness Bay and there was a steamer alongside and dad commented, 'It just shows you how much its rained since yesterday, look where the water has come up to on the side of the steamer. It was way below that red mark yesterday now it is almost up to it.' Cec and I in the back smiled, we knew that the steamer would float up with the water. Dad was looking down at Jean who was sitting in the armrest between them. Jean of course didn't quite understand about the boat rising with the water but sensed that dad was having a little joke and said, 'Oh! You can't fool me!' 'Why not?' Dad said. Then after a second's thought she said, 'Because it was a different steamer!' We all just laughed.

Madge had by now got quite used to looking after us youngest four when mum and dad went home. Most of the time we would be out of the way entertaining ourselves around the farm, just returning for meals when shouted, and then in the evenings after dark we would play games or listen to the wireless. I remember one dark evening when we were all startled by a strange noise coming from outside and we all froze in silence, wondering what it was? The girls huddled up to Madge in fright. There was a rubbing noise against the window followed by heavy breathing and a deep grunting sound, then silence. We looked at each other, hoping that whatever it was had gone away. Then a few minutes later, we heard it again, this time it was in the porch as if it was trying to push the door in. The girls were frantically hanging on to Madge, almost hysterical. Cec had picked up a poker from the fireplace and I armed myself with a small flat iron. We both crept slowly

Bowland Bridge with the Post Office and Toffee Shop on the left
and the Blacksmith's Forge on the right

John Marsh Collection

Fred and Clara Thornborrow when they retired to Ambleside

Ken Thornborrow

up to the door and Cec whipped the curtain back that covered the little square window, to reveal a large pair of staring eyes. We both shouted, 'It's a werewolf!' The girls screamed until we told them, 'Oh no, it's only Blackie!' we said grinning. That was one of Uncle Fred's horses and it had somehow got out of the stables and had been attracted by the light coming from our windows. Cec and I had realised what it was a little earlier, and that was why we were so brave pulling back the curtain.

We've all had many laughs about it since, and also about some of Madge's antics during those early years. I remember her calling us in for our breakfast one morning, and as we sat around the table waiting, she came in from the kitchen wearing one of dad's stiff white collars round her neck, but back to front. She then said in a serious voice, 'Put your hands together and say after me.'

> *The Lound Prayer*
> *Our father*
> *Who art in Radcliffe*
> *Give us this day*
> *Our shredded wheat*
> *And fill our pockets*
> *With lots of pennies*
> *So that we may spend them*
> *In the shop at Bowland*
> *For ever and ever*
> *Oh boy!*

When mum and dad arrived at the weekend, she and Cathy would go down to the village dance on the Saturday night, dad would take them and bring them back when it was over. The first time she went with Cathy she came back with bruised legs, blaming it on the farm boy's hob nailed boots. When dad called her downstairs to say that Cathy had arrived and was ready to go, we heard her shout, 'I'm ready!' Then she came clumping down the oak staircase like an elephant. We all looked round, and there she was, wearing Ellis's football boots and shin pads, with a white tin chamber pot on her head. Everyone just roared with laughter. Dad had tears rolling down his cheeks. Madge was a natural comedian, with her Hilda Baker (comedian) style humour, the life and soul of any party. So as you can imagine, we young ones were always well entertained.

Mum was planning to make bramble jelly during the holidays and was staying over for the second week, so when they arrived they had plenty of empty jam jars and sugar for the occasion. The next day (Sunday) the elder end of the family would be arriving with their future wives and husbands for the day, to help pick the blackberries and spend the rest of the day down at the lake.

When they all arrived in their cars, we all went to pick the blackberries in a little lane above Strawberry Bank. The hedgerows were laden with berries and with many helping hands, the baskets and bowls were soon filled, though us young ones ate more than we picked! We made our way back to the cottage and mother was very pleased with the large amount that had been gathered. She now wanted to be on her own whilst she made the jam, so everyone decided to go down to the lake for the afternoon and leave her unhindered. After a most entertaining afternoon playing games, reluctantly we returned to the cottage, as the day trippers would have to return back home to Radcliffe. It had been a very good day for all the family and mum was always happy in the kitchen making things.

When we arrived back at the cottage Cec and I were the first inside to see how she was doing with the bramble jelly. A lovely fruity smell met us as we entered the front door. There were a few enamel bowls containing the strained juice here and there. As we walked into the kitchen we just stood and looked in amazement at mother, she was standing on a chair pouring a pan of bramble juice into a home made straining contraption she had rigged up over the kitchen sink. It was working alright the juice was straining through into a large white enamel bowl below, but we just stood there pointing and howling with laughter at the object she was straining it through. It was a pair of large pink bloomers that were tied at the top of the legs. The rest of the family joined in laughing and when mum had finished she just smiled and said, 'It's all right they're new ones! I only bought them yesterday on Lancaster Market for your Grandma. She won't mind when they're washed, even if they are a different colour!' Apparently she couldn't find the straining material she's bought but it turned up later, still in the boot of dad's car. So she had improvised the best way she could. Ellis and Archie had the last laugh though, when the strained bramble jelly had cooled enough for pouring into the jars, they had printed all the labels and were sticking them on all the jars. I couldn't read then and wondered what everyone was laughing at, they all read 'Bloomerberry Jelly!' We waved them all off later as they started their journey back home; it had been a wonderful day.

September was to be our last holiday until the following year, Ellis, Archie, mum and dad would be staying over for our last week. Dad would now take them shooting rabbits over Uncle Fred's top fields. There were so many he would be glad to get rid of a few and mum would make a nice stew with them. Dad would let them take a few pot shots with his new .22 Winchester repeating rifle, they loved going out with him. Uncle Fred had shown them how to skin and clean them ready for cooking but Cec and I were of course too young for this kind of sport, we would have to stick to fishing until we were older.

Throughout the daytime for the rest of the week we visited various beauty spots and towns round the area. It had been a wonderful exciting year for us and mum and dad were making sure it finished that way. On the Sunday we said goodbye again to the cottage and stared as we passed by the little toffee shop in Bowland Bridge where we'd walked down with two pennies in our pockets for pop and sweets many times. It would be a long time before we would be able to do the same things again, so we were all feeling sad to leave it all behind but at least there would be many more times in the following years to come.

The rooms above Mr Warburton's shop is where their daughter
taught Audrey and Jean how to dance

Jean 4½ years old

Audrey 11 years old
in 'A Doll Dance'

Chapter Seven

The Dancing Years

Audrey and Jean started attending dancing lessons at the Warburton School of dancing. Our house in Radcliffe was a hive of activity, the girls had taken to it like Cec and I had taken to tickling trout. Evelyn and Rene would make all the stage costumes, so the buzz of sewing machines sounded throughout the house whenever a stage event was to be held, whilst the elder boys would be making many of Jean and Audrey's stage props in the workshop.

Jean, as young as she was had an exceptional talent for music, she could listen to a new song on the radiogram, then run into the front room, jump onto the piano stool and after a few minutes be playing the tune with both hands. I couldn't even play a tune with one finger. She used to sing a song and it summed her up completely:

'Cos I've got a natural talent and I never took a lesson in my life!'

Audrey and Jean went onto the stage doing their own tap and ballet dancing routines during the coming winter months. The whole family took a great interest in the girls' new activity, so there was never a dull moment. I remember well, going to see them at the theatre in Bury where Flanagan and Allen (singing double act – heyday 1930-40s) were the main attraction. Ellis made a large drum for Jean to do her 'toy soldier' tap dancing routine. It had a white marble top, so it gave a good sound effect and looked superb when painted in the traditional colours, finished of with white rope braiding. Jean, resplendent in her toy soldier outfit complemented the scene, as did her act. I saw it on a few occasions and it was quite impressive. Likewise the golden coach dad and Ellis made for a Cinderella Pantomime one Christmas. I would avidly watch them each night as they cut it out with the circular saw. Then finally put it all together and painted it. When the pantomime was staged at our local Coliseum Theatre and picture house, two Shetland ponies were added as the final touch.

Those early winter months seemed to drag for Cec and me as we longed to be at the cottage and in the countryside once more. It couldn't come soon enough for us, but eventually it did come and we would spend each holiday throughout each year with the same enthusiasm as before.

By 1935 Arthur Ransome had moved away from Low Ludderburn and a Mrs Johnson, who had a famous niece called Amy, now owned the cottage. (Amy Johnson was the first woman to fly solo over the Atlantic in 1930 aged twenty-six in her Gypsy Moth aeroplane from England to Australia. She was from Hull in Yorkshire. Sadly a few years later in 1941 she perished in the Thames estuary when the plane she was ferrying crashed. She was seen landing on the water but sadly drowned before being reached.) We young ones didn't know about this until one Sunday, as we passed by Low Ludderburn on our way back from the lake, we saw a magnificent open-top touring car parked at the gate. The spare wheels were mounted at the rear of the front mudguards. I think it was brown, black and cream, with a lot of gleaming chrome work. Then as we all turned our heads and shouted at dad to look, he said, 'Oh! I forgot to tell you about Amy Johnson! That will be her car, her aunty said she would be coming to visit her this weekend!' We were astounded, Amy Johnson, the famous lady aviator here at Low Ludderburn, and we knew nothing about it. Our teacher had been reading to us about her famous solo flight to Australia and Cec had been writing an essay at his school about her too.

When we got back to the cottage, we grabbed a pencil and paper, then ran all the way back to get her autograph. What a story we would be able to tell them all back at school, of actually seeing and speaking to her and getting her autograph as proof. We could hardly believe our luck. Then as Cec and me raced up the last long incline, puffing away and out of breath, we could not see the car radiator coming into view. Maybe she had backed it inside the front yard, but as we finally reached our destination we could see the front yard was quite empty, no sign of her car at all and no sign of anyone around the cottage. We walked back dejected, she must have already been on the point of leaving as we passed by on our way back home and unfortunately she had gone the opposite direction, or we could have waved her down, but it was not to be. Although we always looked out for that lovely car every time we passed, we never did set eyes on it again.

About 1937 dad acquired a small wooden chalet where we kept our boat at Blakeholme on the lakeside. The couple that had owned it had retired and moved to another part of the country. It now meant that instead of transporting everything we needed for the day, we could keep it all there to hand. It had all the basic requirements, water, country toilet, table, chairs, bunk beds, Calor gas stove and lighting. In fact everything required for a prolonged stay and with the little barn at the side, adequate shelter for bicycles and fishing equipment. So now we could shoot off as we wished without too much preparation, and even if it rained we now had a place to shelter and make a meal. It was the perfect retreat, which made our visits down to the lake even more inviting.

In 1937 Johnny, the young man who lived at Hartbarrow Cottage, sadly died after a long illness. His mother decided to leave and go and live at a cottage in Bowland Bridge. Now that her cottage had become vacant (for rent), dad decided to take it, as it was larger and had more than two acres of land, with its own running water and surrounded with damson trees.

We said goodbye to Lound Cottage where we had all shared so many of our early memories and moved quarter of a mile down the road to Hartbarrow Cottage. Now we younger ones had more room to run around and play in our own field, it was just great!

Hartbarrow Cottage

Taken in 1938 at the cottage. Dad, Madge holding nephew Ellis (who had the Fish and Chip shop in Stricklandgate, Kendal in the 1980s) just in front is Jean, then Shirley (Ellis's sister) and me in short pants. Maude, a friend from Radcliffe standing behind.

Chapter Eight

A Taste of Things to Come

By 1939 Cec, who was now working in dad's business, had only one week's summer holiday instead of the three weeks school holidays we'd previously enjoyed together. It wasn't quite as much fun now, although we did spend the odd week or weekend fishing on the lake and in the river, so it came as no surprise to dad when I asked him if I could spend the rest of my holiday helping on a job somewhere. It wouldn't be the same on my own and we'd already had a week at the cottage. So I went back home to sample my first taste of decorating, and this was to be two rows of terraced houses facing each other in the same street.

They were owned by an old lady who lived in the larger house at the end of the street and being an invalid, she was looked after by a housekeeper who saw to all her needs. She had been one of dad's first customers, so the older workmen were quite used to the routine, as they were always painted in the same colours. This was, wood grained doors and windows at the front, light stone gutters all round, brown railings round the front gardens and all green woodwork round the back of the houses. When completed in uniform colours as one unit, they always looked so neat and tidy, but over the years as they became privately owned, they looked a bit like 'a bag of Liquorice Allsorts' as Teddy would say - all different colours!

Cec and myself had the job of cleaning out the front wooden gutters of both rows of houses, about eight on either side. In those days houses had coal fires, so the gutters would be half full of soot. We started the day of with nice clean white overalls and by the end we looked as if we were ready to go on the Black and White Minstrel Show (popular singing and dancing Television show in the 1960s).

As I was the youngest, I was told that I had to attend to the 'brewing up' at ten o' clock. Each time I asked where I was to 'brew up?' I was told, 'You'll find out!' A little chuckle followed, then as it was approaching ten o'clock I was shouted at down the ladder and I was told to follow the dozen or so of them up to the big house at the end of the street.

We entered through the yard where there was a tub of hot water, soap and towel to wash and dry our hands. Then through the kitchen and into quite a large room where Miss Jones, the spinster was sitting in her invalid chair and as we passed by she handed us all a hymn book. So this was what the, 'you'll find out' and chuckling was all about. The secret was out at last – morning service! We arranged ourselves around the room, the housekeeper came in and sat down at the piano, she shouted the hymn number and after a few seconds started to play.

What a noise! Everyone seemed to be out of tune, including me. I still couldn't take in what was happening. When it finished the housekeeper, followed by Teddy and a couple of the older workmen went into the kitchen and brought in mugs of tea and a couple of big platefuls of very welcome 'jam butties'! In the meantime Miss Jones was acquainting herself with those of us she hadn't met before and was pleased to see Cec and me, the youngest two sons in dad's family. When the food and drink was placed on the table Teddy nudged me to wait a bit, apparently we hadn't quite finished. I thought we might have to sing again but with guidance from Teddy we bowed our heads whilst Miss Jones said 'Grace' and then we were able to tuck in! The same routine was repeated each morning until the job was completed and by then the singing had improved so much that I think we would have done well on 'Songs of Praise!'

3rd Sonny   4th Charlie   6th Ellis   7th Archie   10th Ces   11th myself Keith

A band of brothers

Being the boss's son didn't bring any special favours, we were expected to learn and accomplish every job no matter how hard or distasteful it may be and in fact even more so in dad's eyes. At work he was stern but very fair and the men respected him for it.

So painting the iron railings brown, around the fronts of each terraced house was the next job for Cec and me, they seemed never ending like the Firth of Forth Bridge, I know now where the saying, 'I'm browned off' must have originated. They were endless, but fortunately near the end, some of the older improvers who had been painting around the backs, helped finish them off.

Midway through my second week I had a change of jobs. I was to go with my brother Ellis and two other men, Ernie and Syd, to a house in Prestwich about four miles away. The decorating work was near completion, so I was just there to run errands, brew up and just see the work Ellis and the others had done. It was a large detached house standing in its own grounds and was currently unoccupied. Ellis and the other two men had been there for a few weeks, decorating the interior, although there had been other men painting the exterior and that was now finished. As soon as I entered the front door I could see it was something quite special, and as Ellis showed me through each room I knew this was the kind of decorating I wanted to do, painting houses outside was one thing but creative décor was quite something else!

Plastic work as it was called then, was a mixture of Walpamur oil bound water paint and very fine white plaster. This could be patterned with various tools, producing a similar finish to artex. Many of the rooms had been completed in this type of effect but of course in different designs and shades. In those days textured ceilings or walls were intended as a highly decorative finish on perfectly good surfaces rather than a 'cover up' for poor surfaces as it was in the 1970s. This involved a long process. The surface would be painted to seal it. Then the 'plastic work' would be applied and patterned. This was followed by two coats of paint, usually 'off white' eggshell, then finished with a beeswax semi-transparent glaze, which would be tinted to the desired shade.

The large wide staircase looked very impressive with its stone block design, all done in plastic with a deep red lined effect between the imitation blocks. It looked so realistic and attractive even as it was, without the carpet down and furnishings in place.

Each of the downstairs rooms except for the kitchen had been decorated with various designs and colours to tone in with the chosen furnishings. As I was taken through each room my eyes opened wider every time but especially in the nursery that had also been done in a plastic effect. This was of a woodland scene with an embossed fresco of branches and oak leaves running around the top of the wall about eighteen inches (46 cms) in width, with birds and squirrels perched here and there. Then around the wall base ran another fresco of fern leaves, grass, rabbits and other woodland creatures to complete the scene. All these had been shaded in sepia tints along with other delicate shades, then slowly fading into a hint of blue ceiling colour. It all seemed to capture a very early misty morning scene in the Lake District, so it wasn't hard to guess where Ellis had found his inspiration to create this attractive room design.

I wondered how he had managed to form all the embossed leaf, fern, bird and animal shapes. 'Just thick cardboard stencils!' he said and showed me the ones he'd made for the room. Then Ellis explained how after applying them with two or three coats of heavy shellac, it was an easy task to place them in position on the plastic wall surface and apply the plastic mixture, using a wide filling knife, then afterwards finishing the detail with a sculpting knife. It was indeed a work of art and taken a great deal of thinking out, patience and then time spent in the workshop at home where he'd drawn out and made each stencil in his spare time. This was indeed a creation to be proud of and I wondered if I would ever be able to achieve the same high standard of creative décor as Ellis. I could hardly take my eyes off the room. We then went through into a shower room to admire the wall décor at the back of the shower. This was of a waterfall cascading down into a pool of water where two storks were standing and the whole scene had again a misted appearance. This was like a scene from a lavish American film set.

I thought Ellis had painted this on by hand or even with stencils but no, it had been sprayed on through a system of silk screens, using various colours each time until the final completed picture emerged. Ellis had learned this technique at the Leyland Paint and Varnish Company where he went to learn the latest ideas on Creative Décor and having a very artistic nature he was always interested in any new ideas and methods.

The house itself could have been used as a showpiece for various types of effects, which have now long been forgotten. Some of the bedrooms had been decorated in wall-hide, which was again a different type of finish. The idea was to paint the wall in a chosen colour first applying the wall-hide in a lighter shade then various patterns or designs could be created with the background colour partially showing through. I used this many times in later years but this product disappeared completely by the 1960s.

One bedroom in particular really caught my eye, with its deep rose background colour and ivory wall-hide pattern effect. The deep rose background had been shaded into a lighter tint as it ascended the wall, then when patterned over, gave the most stunning effect. Each wall had also been marked out in a large panel with narrow masking tape to form a surrounding border in a different pattern; this really provided the final touch. The 1930s was indeed a very interesting time for decorative effects, people seemed to have more time in those days to spend on finishing off those little extras that make all the difference.

As I walked through each door my attention was drawn to a small metal tube on the door casing, I asked Ellis what they were for and he said, 'Oh! Those are Mazuzzas! Inside each is a little scroll of paper with a Hebrew prayer written thereon. It's the Jewish custom to put their finger to their lips then touch them as they walk through.' This was fascinating I was learning something every minute.

What a lovely house it was and later that afternoon the people who owned it came along to see how the work was progressing. Ellis introduced me to them and said, 'I will always have someone to help me when I'm getting old. He is very interested in the effects!'

It was plain to see the owners were highly delighted with the décor and they came every day now that the work was nearing completion. On the Friday as we were loading the last of the tackle, they brought each of the men a bottle of wine and gave them a very handsome tip, in appreciation for all they had done. I was even included, although I had only been there three days and had contributed little or nothing to the work, apart from running the usual errands, brewing tea, sheeting, cleaning and loading up.

It was now the end of my holidays and I went back to school the following Monday. I had spent the first week of it in the Lake District then the last two helping on jobs, which had been quite educational and given me an insight into what to expect when I would be leaving school in a few more months and with my wages of £1 for the two weeks and a £1 tip I was now quite rich.

The September holidays would soon be here and I was looking forward to it even more, as Cec would have two weeks instead of just the one. Summertime was always dad's busiest time with plenty of outside work to complete. There was always plenty of things to do at the cottage, picking fruit, shooting and fishing, little did we did realise just what was in store for us in the weeks ahead.

Ellis, who was by now twenty-three and planning to marry, came home one day with a loaded trailer but it wasn't full of painting tackle, it was full of furniture, given to him as a wedding present by the people who he was working for. They had been storing it for their German Jewish friends who had sent it over from Nazi Germany prior to them coming over – but they didn't make it.

At that time we weren't to know the reason why, but now of course looking back one can only guess their fate in Hitler's Germany. Ellis was simply told it wouldn't be needed now and to choose whatever he wanted. The large garage was packed with furniture and it would all have to go. I remember a very stylish looking kitchenette, just like new, when we removed the wrapping and let down the working top it had a row of porcelain drawers on the back, each one with German lettering 'Zucker, Salz Pfeffer, Kummel etc (sugar, salt, pepper, caraway seed).

We all wondered why anyone would send over their prized possessions and then not follow on. Maybe they'd had a fatal accident or something? They wouldn't give a reason other than 'it was no longer required.' But now when one sees all the pictures of the Holocaust I wonder just what did happen to those unfortunate people who owned the furniture, and I shudder to think!

Radcliffe Central Senior School built in 1932

Chapter Nine

Schooldays

School life was a very enjoyable experience for me, from start to finish. I remember the day I first started, I was only four, but from that day on I would always look forward to going to the little school at the top of the street where we lived, Saint John's Primary School, where I would attend with Cec until I was eleven.

Each morning we would eagerly await the milk deliveries when every pupil was given a small gill bottle (¼ pint) complete with straw. The school building was in two parts but joined together in the centre by a small covered passage. This kept the younger children separate from the older pupils and was a good arrangement, as every afternoon in the younger children's hall, it was 'nap time' where we would lie down on mattresses for a half hour or so. We had a large rocking horse with a cart and we would all take turns to sleep in this during our time in the kiddies half and had been donated by Doctor Flack who lived in our street.

Dad often gave Cec and me old wallpaper pattern books to take into school and the younger classes would use them for creative art lessons. Once you went into the older half of the school, teaching became a little more serious and interesting. I liked the lady teachers, who sometimes spent part of their holidays in groups together, like the time one Easter when I was playing in the front garden at Hartbarrow Cottage and saw this group of people walking down the lane. I thought they all looked familiar, but no it couldn't be, not in this part of the world! In those days seldom did one travel more than a few miles from home. As they drew nearer there was no mistaking who they were, my present teacher Miss Partington, Miss Brombley, Miss Rothwell and two others who had also been my teachers. I stood there gaping, wondering why they had come such a distance, surely not for something I'd done at school! Miss Partington smiled and said, 'Hello Keith! So this is where you spend you holidays, how lovely! Are you parents in?' I just said, 'Yes!' It transpired that they were on a walking holiday and were staying at the Hare and Hounds in the village and had asked the way to our cottage, so they could call and say 'hello!'

So after tea, coffee and biscuits and much laughter from inside the cottage they went on their way again. At the end of the week they paid us another visit and we all went down the lane leading to the river and then into a small rocky field covered with daffodils. Dad must have had a word with the farmer for permission to dig up a few wild daffodil bulbs for school and to everyone's delight they had been transplanted into bowls when we returned, adorning every windowsill. The children were told the story of how they had come by them, I felt quite embarrassed at the time!

Though this was somewhat surpassed on a later occasion when I should have been concentrating on the lesson chalked up on the blackboard and what the teacher was explaining in detail to the class. It was all about the big industrial towns of England beginning with the letter 'B' examples being – Bolton, Bury, Birmingham, Barrow, Burnley – but I was more interested in the comic I was reading behind my exercise book. I was reading the last chapter of a cowboy serial I had been following for weeks and I couldn't wait to find out how it had ended, I think it was the 'Adventure' comic. It was about a character called 'The Silver King' - exciting stuff and it was the showdown at last! I was still in Eldorado when the boy in the next desk nudged me and said, 'Teacher wants you!'

I quickly looked up to discover the whole class looking at me and the teacher, Miss Partington standing at her desk looking over the top of her glasses at me, 'Come here and bring your exercise book with you!' she said sharply. I was sitting in the back row, tucked away in the furthest corner from her, so it seemed like an eternity when I made my way to the front. She held her hand out for my exercise book and looked inside. 'I think you will know more about Buffalo Bill than the industrial B's we've been talking about. Can you tell me which is the biggest industrial B of them all?' I quickly said, 'The Bumble Bee Miss! At that the whole class erupted in a loud outburst of laughter that I'm sure must have been heard throughout the school. When the laughter had died down, the teacher pointed to the blackboard and said with a smile on her face, 'A very good answer but not quite the one we were looking for. It should have been Birmingham!'

I had to sit at the front of the class for the rest of the day with a very red face and had to put up with many strange buzzing sounds and titters whenever the teacher left the classroom. My comic that had been confiscated, was returned to me at home time with the teacher saying, I'm sure you won't bring your comics to read in school anymore. She was right, it was a lesson well learnt.

When we came back after the summer holidays our teacher told us about her holiday in Germany and how they ate what they called 'black bread' with 'Ersatz' margarine, we thought this sounded awful. Our bread was always white and we couldn't understand why the German people ate such terrible stuff, until she explained that all the white flour grain and butter was for export only. She went on to say that everywhere she travelled on the buses and trains, large placards could be seen saying 'Guns before Butter' but we were only ten at that time and didn't quite understand the significance of these sinister messages, but a few years later we certainly would.

My last year at St. John's School was very enjoyable indeed, Mr Bullock the headmaster was very keen on football and I had been chosen to play on the school team. Over the past few years the schools' cup had always been won by St. John's and he was very proud of that. But with players like Eddie Quigley, who was later to play for the big professional teams and Johnny Morris, his nephew, who was later to play for Manchester United, how could he lose. When they left school Mr Bullock was a little apprehensive about his new team that included a few of the younger brothers of his prize team, that had won just about everything. Needless to say it was football practise at morning, lunchtime and afternoon break and sometimes evenings as well. I think he was trying to out best his brother, who was the then manager of Bury Football Club and I often wondered why he didn't arrange a match with them. To his obvious delight we sailed through every game and preserved the school record once again, but how could we lose when he'd produced another excellent captain in Sammy Makin, who we considered to be in the same category as his previous stars. In 1937 his next team didn't quite make it in the final and Mr Bullock's reign came to an end, after that it was never the same for him.

The new school Radcliffe Central Senior School was 'out of this world' even by modern standards, a pleasure to attend! It had been built in 1932 just a year or two before; Cec was probably one of the first pupils to attend this ultra modern school, with its four lawned quadrangles, art rooms, woodwork and metalwork rooms, two large assembly halls, science rooms, large classrooms with long sliding (green faced) blackboards and internal telephones on the walls.

The school was divided into two, one half for the boys and the other for girls each having their own facilities and being taught by masters and mistresses respectively. There was even a dental surgery that was built in the far corner of the school grounds where we had to attend regularly for inspection. We always commented that the reason it was situated there was so that we couldn't hear the screams!

The sports facilities were fabulous – ample football pitches, practise pitches, and hockey pitches for the girls; it was indeed a modern model school. Competition too was encouraged between the various house colours. For the boys there was; Derby, Kay, Peel and Scott and for the girls; Nightingale,

Beaufort, St. Hilda and Fry, all named after famous or eminent people. This encouraged them to win points for their own particular house awarded in all subjects.

When eventually, I did leave this wonderful school, it was with very mixed feelings. The past ten years had been a very pleasant experience – good schools, teachers and pals, now I would have to leave it all behind. How uncertain the future looked, not because of the shortage of work opportunities, everyone leaving school in those days had a job to go to before they left. No, it was the realisation that war was upon us and things were getting tougher, rationing, blackouts, conscription, shortages and Dunkirk. No one knew what the future held. I knew however that I would be working in dad's business.

During the war a Doddlebug (V1 Flying Bomb) blew up a small boat-building yard two hundred yards (metres) away from the school. The school windows were damaged and an extra week's holiday.

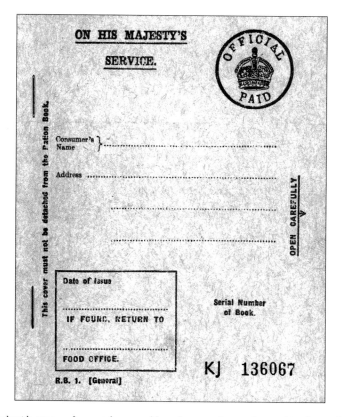

Ration book with coupons for meat, bacon and ham, butter and margarine, cooking fats, including lard and dripping and last, but not least, sugar   Imperial War Museum (Martha Bates)

Chapter Ten

Second World War

The September holidays of 1939 were dramatically cut short with the realisation that we were now at war with Nazi Germany. I remember we all crowded round our accumulator powered wireless set in Hartbarrow Cottage to hear the Prime Minister, Mr Neville Chamberlain announce the dreaded statement. I don't think we youngest ones fully realized just how serious the situation was, but the older ones knew that it would soon mean conscription into the armed forces and the look on everyone's faces said it all.

Both mum and dad had planned to stay with us all for that first week, but they decided to go back home to find out what was expected of everyone, with the instructions that we had to phone them from the village every evening.

By the end of the week we had learnt that blackout restrictions were in force, barrage balloons floated over power stations, concrete air raid shelters were being built, Air Raid Precaution (ARP Wardens) were being recruited and everywhere was in a state of upheaval. Dad told us that as they travelled back home on the Sunday night, they had met processions of vehicles fleeing the towns, loaded with people and belongings tied to the car roofs.

Wartime – at Hartbarrow Cottage with Dad (right) and Frank Barnes. He lived in Radcliffe and helped run his father's small factory – 'Entwistle's Pickles' – also made jams. He would have been collecting seasonal fruits to take back with him. Note the blackout covers on front lights.

Obviously panic had gripped many people and those who owned a vehicle were making for the countryside.

We had already blacked out our cottage windows and there was little else we could do but wait and see what was going to happen next. Two weeks later dad came up and took all of us youngest ones home again, as the immediate threat of being bombed at this time had passed.

Jean and I went back to school with gas masks that we would carry everywhere. Air raid shelters had been hastily constructed and rationing was now beginning too. Everyone was encouraged to grow vegetables. There was a big plot at the back of the school and that provided most of the vegetables for the school kitchen. The school gardener helped to teach the boys to produce as much as possible. Many women were conscripted to take the place of the men in munitions or war equipment factories, so it was the girl pupils' lesson to cook all the school dinners, under the supervision of one cook. The result was excellent and something we would all look forward to every day. It was the boys' job to do the washing up afterwards, in turn of course. Nobody really minded this, as our reward was an extra portion of whatever was left over. The dinners cost 5d. (2p) per day, or if for the full week 1s. 9d. (9p).

Early in 1940 rationing was put in force and many things we had taken for granted were now becoming harder to obtain. Fortunately dad always kept a large stock of paint and wallpaper materials in-hand, but of course no one knew how long the war would last, so it was a matter of conserving them for as long as possible.

In those days it was the practice to mix one's own paint from very thick stiff paste colours. These came in very large wooden barrels, zinc white, Venetian red, yellow ochre, burnt and raw Sienna, amber, green, blue and so on. The old time tradesman would mix his own requirement accordingly, whether it was undercoating, eggshell, semi-gloss, or gloss, by adding substitute turps (turpentine) and linseed oil and a little paint drier (terebine).

In the workshop there were two very large tanks holding about five hundred gallons in each, raised about two feet from the ground with a tap fitted at the base for the workmen to fill their empty boiled linseed oil or turpentine cans up with. Two smaller tanks contained raw linseed oil and terebine. Raw linseed oil was added to the graining scumble rather than boiled, as it allowed the grainer a little more time to manipulate or form the scumble to the desired effect.

Various dry colours in powder form would be kept in a long wooden chest; these would be supplied in strong one hundredweight paper bags from the manufacturer. These were emptied into different compartments as required. Whiting would be thinned into a milky or creamy consistency first, and then tinted with the powder colours, according to shade. During the war this was used extensively for ceiling finishes, but of course was unsuitable for wall surfaces, as it would brush off on contact with your clothing.

So for wall surfaces, glue size would be added to bind the mixture when it dried, this was called distemper and again used extensively as a cheap form of décor, before and during wartime. Oil bound washable water paints had become unobtainable, as were many other materials containing valuable oils.

During the 1930s Cec and me would help our elder brothers and the workmen to load and unload the working materials from trailers and handcarts, putting them all in their correct places, or helping to get together materials for the particular job they were working on. By the time we started work we were well acquainted with all these materials, all we really needed to know was how to use them, and of course we had excellent teachers.

By the end of my schooldays the war had been in progress for a few months and manpower was becoming a problem. I remember one young teacher being called up into the RAF very soon after the war started, and twelve months later we heard had been killed in action. Then our sports master was called up soon after, so it was a case of masters having to double up on lessons.

Mr Ogden the geography master had been gassed in the First World War and would possibly have retired but stayed on, although it was plain to see it had badly affected him. Often his face would turn a greenish colour and he would cough agonisingly into his handkerchief. At this point he would appoint a prefect to take over, then he would go out into the quadrangle for ten minutes until it had cleared. This war had made us all realise what he had to endure and no one took advantage of his handicap by teasing him.

Dad had taken on the job of painting two nearby sweet works – Halls (Mentho Lyptus) and Fittons, both at Whitefield. This would help to keep the older tradesmen busy and help to conserve our un-replaceable material stocks, as priority was given for the painting of certain factories supplying essential goods, and confectionary supplies fell under this category for both civilian and the Forces requirements.

When I left school and started working for dad many of his workforce had already been 'called-up' into the Armed Forces including my older brothers, Charlie, Ellis and Archie. Fortunately for me I had already had a sample of apprentice work the year before, so I knew what to expect

Archie, the youngest, was the first casualty. It was around the time of Dunkirk, when we received word that he had been badly injured and would be an invalid for the rest of his life. Archie had to wear a plaster jacket for about two years, then after many operations a metal plate was inserted into his back. A removable jacket of aluminium and leather allowed him at least to sleep easier each night.

I now realized some of my mother's fears. Archie had told me how mother had broken down one Sunday evening before the war had started, when she had answered a knock at the front door. Charlie was standing there in uniform proudly displaying his pilot's wings. The sudden shock of seeing him in uniform caused her to break down in tears. She hated uniforms. Cec and I knew nothing of this as we were at the cottage with dad but when Archie told me years later, we realized just why she hated uniforms.

When I was very young she had shown me a photograph of her brother Albert, who had been killed in the First World War. Then she went on to tell me that when her mother opened a parcel containing his personal belongings, she had discovered a letter she had written to him soaked in bloodstains. When I told Archie about this he didn't speak for a few minutes then said quietly, 'Poor mother!' What must have been in her thoughts, to see all six of us in uniform?

Charlie like dad was quite a daredevil on a motorbike and must have been in his element when the Government in October 1938 offered to subsidise Air Training facilities to all Civil Flying Clubs in the United Kingdom. In all fifty-seven clubs opted to take part in the scheme, so the Civil Air Guards were formed. Charlie did his training at Barton Aerodrome, near Manchester each weekend and kept this secret from the family intending it as a surprise when he earned his wings and mother had burst into tears when she answered the door that Sunday. So his spirits must have been greatly dampened with her reaction and even more so, when later he was called up into the Royal Air Force and not accepted for flying duties in spite of his flying experience. Possibly this was because he had two young children, who knows? With his daredevil outlook I always thought he would have made a good fighter pilot.

As the war progressed, petrol rationing prevented us from travelling to the cottage except on very special occasions. Dad now had a much smaller car,

Cec had a little two-stroke motorcycle and I had my bicycle. Most of dad's work force was now under eighteen (conscription age) but as soon as their birthdays arrived they would be 'called-up' into the Forces.

Teddy was dad's oldest workman and I became his apprentice, working with him throughout the week. Then at the sweet works each weekend when the factory was closed down. This was of course the only time many departments could be decorated. Having a sweet tooth I would look forward to this, as the sweet ration at that time was only three ounces (75 g) a week, and anyone who worked there could eat as many sweets as they liked, which everyone did initially. After a few days the temptation would wear off and many of the workforce would be almost sick at the sight of the binfulls of sweets they had to handle each day, fortunately this didn't happen to me.

We had transformed both sweet works from being very drab looking places of work, into gaily coloured departments, and was very much appreciated by the workforce. The ceilings and walls had been whitewashed, with dark green painted dado and a black line dividing the two. Now everywhere was sunshine yellow, with black and red lines above the dado. All the pipes had been painted in bright colours, blue, orange, red, silver and so on, depending on the type of supply it provided.

It was good to see their faces when they returned to work after they had been on holiday to discover a completely different atmosphere, loudspeakers had been installed and 'Music While You Work' played along in the background. All this of course was designed to keep the people's spirits up as we were indeed going through some very hard times. One could hardly walk down the street without hearing of someone's husband or son being killed in action.

There was a very strong bond in those days between people, we had our backs to the wall and everyone knew it only too well and had it not been for the leadership and defiance of Winston Churchill it could well have been a very different story indeed.

I remember only too well the bombing in Manchester in early December 1940 (four nights on the run) and the gloating 'Lord Haw Haw' (William Joyce) on the radio as he boasted about their mastery of the sky and how we were powerless to do anything about it. He was quite right of course but he should have remembered the phrase 'He who laughs last laughs the longest!' In the end Lord Haw Haw learned the hard way – at the end of a rope! He was hanged for treason on 3rd January 1946.

That first night when the air raid sirens sounded in Manchester, followed by the deep droning of the German bombers, the loud thud of bombs and landmines hitting buildings in and around the city must have been terrifying for many as it went on and on. Cec and I watched outside as the searchlights fanned the sky, then suddenly a German bomber would be caught in a beam like a moth caught in the light of a torch. Half a dozen other searchlights would lock on to it, then anti-aircraft guns would blaze away sending a shower of shrapnel clattering down on the slate roof tops in the surrounding streets. Cec and I stood there holding metal dustbin lids over our heads, when an Air Raid Warden shouted to us to get under cover. I went inside to report what we had seen, dad was still in bed, nothing ever seemed to ruffle him, his philosophy was, 'If it's got your name on it, it will get you no matter where you are!'

Mother and Jean were both sheltering in a cupboard under the stairs; it was quite cool in there. Mother used it to store her flour and sugar, and eggs that dad had preserved in a big bowl of 'Isinglass'. As I opened the door I could see them both crouching down, huddled in mother's fur coat. I told them what was happening and that the bombs weren't actually falling too near us, but they wouldn't come out, they were too frightened, so I went back to see what was happening just in time to see a German bomber drop a magnesium flare. The whole sky seemed to light up, then a tremendous barrage of 'ack ack' guns let loose.

The nearest anti-aircraft gun was situated about three quarters of a mile from us as the crow flies, and the shrapnel clattered down on the rooftops again, just as if a few dozen-mill girls were hurrying down the street in their iron-shod clogs. One bomb did sound very loud indeed, almost as if it was at the top of the street, the house shook a little, and it must have scared mother and Jean out of their wits, but then after a while the drone of the bombers faded, they had dropped their bombs and were now returning home.

Cec and I looked south over Manchester where the sky glowed red, and then to our right in the distance we could see another red glow. Liverpool had caught it. The all clear sounded. Inside, mother and Jean were emerging from their hiding place. It had been a terrifying ordeal for them as it was for thousands of families up and down the country.

The next morning Cec and I were both up early searching for souvenirs, we found quite a lot of shrapnel scattered around, and many damaged greenhouses to repair. Mother mentioned at breakfast that they would have to make it more comfortable under the stairs. Dad having his little joke said,

'It's a good job they didn't drop one nearer, or you might have come out, battered in more ways than one!' (Milk, flour and eggs were stored there).

Audrey and Madge had been on shift work during the attack, making tank parts, but had been evacuated into the air raid shelters when the sirens sounded and had spent half the night wondering how we were faring. So they were relieved to find we were all right and the house was still standing.

Both Cec and myself made ourselves available for fire watch duties at the sweet works after the bombing, as did all dad's other young men who had not yet received their 'call-up' papers.

My sister Rene's husband was a senior ARP Warden whilst she organised parcels for the servicemen abroad. Evelyn's husband Sydney was in the Coldstream Guards in North Africa, whilst she helped Rene. Madge's husband Freddy was in the Ordinance Corps in Egypt, whilst she and Audrey worked on vehicle components for the army. Harold, Audrey's husband, was doing highly classified work for the Government and so was reluctantly exempt from active service.

Chapter Eleven

Cowslips and Bullrushes

Early in 1941, dad wanted to visit the cottage to see that everything was alright, so Cec and I went with him for a long weekend, it was good to see the logs burning in the fire again. We spent the few days fishing and shooting. Rabbit was a good way to supplement the meat ration and I remember we had quite a few to take back with us, to be shared amongst ourselves, friends and neighbours.

We took the boat out for a day's fishing and then stowed it away again in the little barn for future use. We aired the chalet and made everything secure again and had managed to catch a few fish into the bargain which we gave to the local farmers. The following day we went shooting in the morning and decided to go fishing in the river after lunch. We were making the most of our visit whilst we could as our trips to the cottage were now few and far between, due to petrol rationing.

We went down the road to the little river that flowed along through the Winster Valley – wending its way through Bowland Bridge. Cec and I went upstream, using our hands to catch the fish, whilst dad worked his way

Cec rowing on Windermere

down stream, with his rod and fishing gear. After Cec and me had caught a dozen or so trout, we decided to go back to the cottage and prepare them for tea.

On the way back as we turned a bend we saw a figure climbing over the gate ahead of us, it was dad, looking bedraggled, with no hat, glasses, rod or basket and dripping wet through. We caught up with him and asked, 'What had happened?' All we could get out of him was, 'That blasted bull!' Cec and I looked at each other and guessed the rest.

We hurried back up the hill to the cottage and got dad changed before he caught cold, as it was quite a cold day and he was shivering like a jelly. When he'd changed and warmed up with a hot drink, he told us what had happened. He had been fishing for a while, moving downstream and had actually caught one, then decided to move further down to another position. It was quite a large field with part of it hidden by a wood, he'd noticed a few cows in the field and one a bit nosier than the rest. This one had made its way over to him and kept nosing his basket on the ground. He had shooed it off a couple of times but it kept persisting, so he flicked it with his rod.

The cow turned sharply and slipped on its side with a loud 'moo' and the next he knew was seeing a bull charging across the field bellowing away, so he dived over the hedge into the river on the other side. Luckily he had chosen a place to fish where the river was just a little deeper at that point so he hadn't landed on any rocks, but of course he had lost his hat and glasses in the process and got soaked through.

Cec and I went down to the river to see if we could find them, the bull was over the other side of the field with the cows so Cec waded over and managed to get through the hedge, then passed dad's rod and tackle over to me, his glasses we found in the hedge and his trilby about twenty yards down stream.

I suppose it was one of those incidents you could laugh about afterwards but at the time it had been a very close shave for dad – we learned later the farmer who owned it, Bert Moon, was badly gored by it. Normally the bull was kept in its own field with a high wall around it, on a length of the river where Cec and I had fished. It was indeed a very bad tempered bull, often we would climb onto the bridge wall and peer over, then when it saw us, it would charge over snorting and bellowing away. However the long weekend passed away without further incidents and we reluctantly returned home looking forward to the next visit, whenever that would be.

Charlie in his RAF uniform

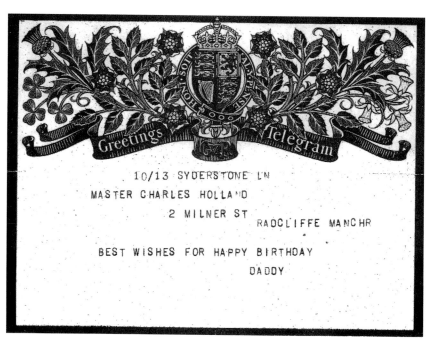

Greetings telegram

10/13 SYDERSTONE LN
MASTER CHARLES HOLLAND
2 MILNER ST
RADCLIFFE MANCHR

BEST WISHES FOR HAPPY BIRTHDAY
DADDY

The telegram Charlie sent to his son

Chapter Twelve

Sad Times

It was midsummer time, in 1941 when Cec and I were both working outside on a house with Teddy, who was by now the only tradesman left in dad's decorating business. I remember that day only too well, dad called round to see how the job was progressing or so we thought, but he didn't come through the gate, just beckoning Teddy over to him.

They spoke for about ten minutes, then dad left, when Teddy came back, he was quiet and solemn and then finally blurted out, 'It's your brother Charlie, missing presumed killed!' He put his arms around our shoulders, and said, 'I think you'd better finish what you're doing and go home. Your dad was too upset to tell you himself, he's got to go home and break the bad news to your mother.' Teddy turned away wiping the tears from his eyes. He had taught Charlie as an apprentice when he had first started work, just like Cec and me, so the news had affected him deeply, there had been a close bond between Teddy and my elder brothers throughout the 1920s and 30s.

Cec and I got on our bikes and made our way home, not wanting to get there and see mother in a bad state, or dad trying to hide his emotions so we went to my sister Rene's house first which was in the opposite direction. She too had heard the tragic news from Charlie's wife who lived nearby; that his ship had been torpedoed by a German submarine whilst on its way to South Africa. Everyone was in a state of shock and disbelief.

When we did eventually get home we were both relieved to find that dad had taken mother to stay overnight at her sisters in Pendleton, I don't think any of us were in a fit enough state to comfort her.

Later when I visited Beatrice, Charlie's wife, she lent me his record collection, all the comical George Formby ones, which was typical of Charlie who had a very jovial nature. Then as I took one out of its sleeve a letter dropped out, it turned out to be a letter from me when I was seven years old, it read, Dear Challi (my incorrect spelling), then went on thanking him for the nice present he'd bought me on my birthday. It was a typical children's letter with amusing spelling mistakes, which was probably why he'd kept it. I smiled when I read it and was thankful I was by myself at the time.

We would probably never have known the exact details of what had really happened to Charlie had it not been for my nephew Darrell, Archie's eldest son, and eventually the whole story finally came to light. A few years ago Darrell who lives in the Cheltenham area, quite by chance went into a bookshop. The first book he picked up was displaying the picture of the ship Charlie had been on when it was torpedoed, this he knew from RAF records. He said, 'He didn't know what made him go into the shop and straight to the book it was if he'd been drawn to it.' Since then he has discovered many more facts about the incident, even relating to the U-Boat commander and the U-Boat involved, and even more incredible for me was whilst I was writing about how we would never know the true facts of how Charlie met his fate the postman pushed all the information through the letter box.

The Anselm, the ship that Charlie had been on, was 5.954 GRT, 412ft (125.6m) length, 55 ft (16.7m) beam, steam turbine, single screw, 14kts. She was operated by the Booth Line (William Denny, Dunbarton) and operated a cargo and passenger service to South America from Liverpool until the start of the Second World War, when she was taken over for service as an auxiliary transport. We learn of that last fateful voyage thanks to the writings of two persons aboard. Firstly from a chaplain (no further details):

'We sailed from Gourock (in Scotland) in a convoy of troopships. The convoys zig-zagged to avoid being torpedoed, but being in the tail-end of the convoy we were torpedoed by a German U-boat in the early hours of Saturday, July 6 1941, three hundred miles off the Azores and six days out of England. We clambered into the lifeboats as best we could, only to be told to jump out to avoid being dragged down by the Ship's suction. It sank in twenty-five minutes. After swimming for a while we were picked up by three of the Navy escort ships. We were told afterwards that we had been in shark-infested waters! Two hundred and twenty-four men were lost out of a compliment of about thirteen hundred. The tragedy was that the staircase of the lower deck was blown away and many of the men could not swim. I was hauled up on the deck of the Naval survey ship. My tunic and trousers dried in the Captain's Cabin. Very soon I was called upon to take three funerals, remembering the essential parts of the service by heart, as all my books and belongings were at the bottom of the sea and there was no Book of Common Prayer on the Bridge. We were then transferred, at sea, to the Armed Merchant Cruiser 'Cathay' and put into Freetown, West Africa, to re-kit.'

Further details come from Dave Everett of Penn, Wolverhampton (from an article in the News and Star, West Midlands) and relates to the troopship being escorted from Scotland by the destroyer 'Challenger' leading up to when it was torpedoed and sunk in twenty-five minutes and witnessing the astonishing heroism of a Midlands Padre.

'I remember scanning the bulletin board, six days later: For the attention of all

servicemen, *'Pyjamas can be worn now that we are out of the danger area.'* A matelot with a stiff beard behind me growled: *That must have been written by a U-boat Commander!* *Is there a safe place anywhere in the Atlantic?*

He continues by saying that he was part of a boxing team and used to keep fit by running round the deck as he was doing at 5 am that particular morning when the torpedo struck. He writes of the chaos and panic he witnessed. The screams and howls of men trapped below. The Challenger nosed closer to the back of the ship catching servicemen dropping onto the stern. He mentions that there was a discrepancy in losses – figures ranging from 250 to over 500.

He tells of the amazing bravery of Padre Pugh:

'Padre Pugh, the first padre at the RAF Bridgnorth Station, was haggling with a couple of erks (aircraftmen) to lower him down so that he could bring solace to the doomed erks trapped below. His last words were: My love of God is greater than my fear of death!'

Some years later he heard that Padre Pugh had been awarded the George Cross posthumously for his bravery. Dave goes on to say that he met another survivor who had witnessed the RC Priest's bravery in sacrificing his life and had converted to Catholicism. He goes on to write:

'The irony being that it was a mistake. Padre Pugh was Church of England. He had shared a cabin with a Catholic Priest and in the pandemonium, each had donned the wrong tunic!'

The correct details of the brave man of God is:

The Rev. Herbert Cecil Pugh (1898-1941) was awarded the George Cross posthumously in April 1947. The official citation says he was last seen 'kneeling with the men in prayer as the ship sank.'
This certainly brings home to us the great sacrifice these brave men made for us!

We also discovered that the commander of the U-96 submarine responsible for sinking SS Anselm was Kaptit. Heinrich Lehmann-Willenbrock. He was so successful in his U-boat that within a short span he had sunk 125,580 tons of our shipping. The German war correspondent, Sonderfuhrer-Leutnant Lothar-Gunther Buchheim accompanied the U-96 on her seventh patrol and thirty years later he wrote the book 'Das Boot' of his experiences and Lehmann-Willenbrock served as the model for the commander in it. Lehmann- Willenbrock died in 1986 aged 75 years old.

Ellis in 1942 – in RAF flying kit

Chapter Thirteen

Brothers in Arms

Christmas time 1941, was a time of austerity, no new toys in the shops and the few that were, would be 'painted up second hand ones.' Archie said he knew where he could get some toy soldier moulds, and could Cec and I make some forts? His idea was to sell them for a bit of spare money at Christmas, he had been talking to the Co-op manager who said, 'He'd nothing to display in his store when Christmas came.' So all November and December up until Christmas Cec and I were busy in the workshop, whilst Archie was busy at his home, moulding and painting toy soldiers. He was prevented from doing more owing to his war injury.

Dad let us take down much of the plywood that had covered the workshop ceiling, that would have been taken down after the war was over and replaced with asbestos sheeting for fire protection. With a circular saw and plenty of paint to hand, Cec and I set about making our Christmas toys. Dad helped us with advice and design, we had a whole mixture of wooden toys scattered around the workshop ranging from castles, tanks, dolls cots and a few farmyards. Archie had also managed to find a mould for the animals too.

It really is surprising what a bit of paint can do, even on second hand timber. Then when they were finally displayed in the shop window everything sold in two days, and the manager was asking for more but of course this was impossible in the short time left.

Archie with a big smile on his face came hobbling into the workshop holding some pound notes in his hand, which were to be our share. Cec and I had already decided long before, that it was to be his Christmas present as we could earn extra money doing fire watch duty at the sweet works; besides we didn't have any children to buy for.

Cec and I had enjoyed making the toys; it had given us something worthwhile to do. We were pleased with what we'd achieved. Dad was the only loser, he'd lost the inner lining of his workshop ceiling, provided the paint and had to pay for the extra electricity, but we knew he didn't mind at all, he was just very thankful to see us at home and not in uniform.

In April 1942, Cecil was 'called-up' into the Forces, Teddy had also been conscripted too so now there was only dad and myself left to try to keep the business going for when Ellis and Cec returned home. Sonny would have no partner now that Charlie wouldn't be coming home, so the effects of war were now beginning to bite deeply.

It was one Tuesday evening in the following July, I know it was Tuesday because that was the night the Coliseum didn't show pictures, instead it was variety night. Once a week mother and father would go along to watch the show in which Jean was appearing.

I was at home in the workshop with the house door open listening in case the telephone should ring. Dad and I had been working at a house near Prestwich, where Ellis had worked. The room we were decorating had suffered one or two cracks on the walls as a result of a bombing raid, so we were now making them good and repainting the room. It had been decorated in plastic (similar to artex) but in those days was composed of Walpamur and fine plaster.

Ellis had 'stencilled on' a motif of a jumping gazelle over the chimney breast, and the same one had to be applied again. Back in the workshop I had managed to find the same stencil Ellis had used, but it was damaged and needed replacing, I was busy making another one when I heard the phone ring, so I dashed in to answer it. At first I couldn't make out what the lady on the other end was trying to say, she was obviously upset, and sobbing. She wanted to know was dad in? I explained where they had gone, and could she leave a message. It was Ellis's mother-in-law and in between sobs she managed to get out, 'Ellis is missing and presumed killed!'

I was stunned. I just couldn't say anything. She went on to say, 'That they'd been hit returning from a mission over Germany and the last they'd heard was, that they were coming down over the North Sea.' Ellis was the wireless operator and he would have sent the message but they didn't make it. She then went on to say that Dorothy his wife had given birth to a baby boy 'Tony' a week or so before. Ellis had held the baby in his arms 'just once' before his last fateful mission.

When I put the phone down I was completely shaken. First it was Archie, then Charlie, and now Ellis. How was I going to tell Dad? I knew I couldn't tell mother and then I thought about the stencil Ellis had made. Why had all this got to happen? My mind was in a whirl, what to do? Poor mother and dad, should I go around to the Coliseum two streets away? No, it would only spoil the night for them but they would have to know sooner or later. In the end I decided to wait for them to come home when the show had finished and then tell dad. I went back into the workshop to finish the stencil, but I couldn't face it. Suddenly I heard the garage door slide back, it was dad coming in, he went into the office to get something, and I shouted to him that there had been a phone call, but he was rushing out again as I came down the steps from the loft above. 'Not now!' he was answering, 'It's the interval, I have to get back!' I shouted again, and when he turned he could see there was something very wrong. I said, 'It's Ellis!' I think he'd already guessed, his face went ashen as he closed the garage door, then we went inside and sat down whilst I told him.

Dad leaned forward with his head in his hands; I knew how much Ellis had meant to him, not only as a son, but in the business too. Two sons missing and a third one disabled, where was it all going to end? Dad had let it be known that when Ellis returned he would like us all to be working in the business together. Archie would look after the office and dad and mum would retire to the cottage.

Dad got up wearily from the armchair with tearful eyes and said, 'I'd better get back before they wonder what has happened to me.' As we opened the front door he put his arm round my shoulder and pulled me tight. He didn't like to show emotion, so I knew how hard the news had hit him. As he went through the door he just said, 'Don't let your mother know anything tonight, I'll tell her tomorrow.'

I went to bed early but heard them return with one or two friends, I could hear them laughing and joking about the entertainment. I knew dad must have been falling apart inside. It had taken a long time before mother had accepted the loss of Charlie and now it was Ellis, dad would be dreading the dawn.

It was a long time before I got to sleep that night, but I awakened the following morning, remembering the terrible phone call the night before. It wasn't a day to look forward to, but I had to avoid Jean and Audrey and most of all mother. So I got up, had a quick breakfast, put up my lunch and went into the workshop to wait for dad.

I knew what he had in mind, so I was prepared to carry on with the work alone until dad had broken the news to mother. When he came out he just said, 'I'll take you to work and explain what's happened to the lady. Can you carry on, on your own?' I said, 'Yes, I'll be alright.' I knew I would be that day, because it was only plain background painting. Dad explained to the lady, who was deeply distressed, as Ellis had worked there many times before. Dad said he would try to get back and then travelled home in the car.

Audrey and Jean were home when I arrived, but dad had taken mother to be with her sisters as before, she was going to stay a few days until she'd got over the shock. The house was silent, as never before, no one knew what to say or do for the best. Dad was in shock too and in no fit state to carry on at work that week. He had many other things to do and I didn't relish the thought of working in the same room for his sake or mine. There were too many things in the room to remind him of Ellis, so he would take me each morning, make sure I could manage on my own then leave me to it. I would travel home on the bus.

So, it was 'On with the Motley' (line of a popular song), the paint and the anguish. I had much to do, which was just as well; it was impossible even for one second to think of anything else except my brothers. My mind would slip back to when Cec and I were both very young, in happier times, how they would play or gently tease us both, Sonny, Charlie, Ellis and Archie, giving Cec and myself an aeroplane ride, blindfolded and sitting on a board! They would raise us off the ground gently swirling us around, then tell us we were climbing into the clouds, and to mind we didn't fall off, or bang our heads on the ceiling. Then when we did feel a gentle bump on our heads, the board we were on would tilt to one side amid shouts of 'Look out you're falling!' I remember a feeling of short-lived panic as we fell softly onto the cushions laid on the carpet below. Actually they had lifted us less than a foot of the ground and the ceiling we thought we'd bumped our heads on proved to be no more than two books 'tapped' on our heads!

By the end of the week the room was completed to the satisfaction of all, including the 'jumping gazelle' stencil effect, in spite of all the grief and unsure ness in my mind.

Darrell (my nephew), later discovered the facts, Ellis's plane had been on a bombing mission over Hamburg, in Germany. We always thought he flew in a Wellington bomber but apparently the plane was a Halifax with a crew of seven. He discovered all the details including the names of the other crewmembers (Royal Air Force Bomber Command Losses of the Second World War [Vol 3 Aircraft and Crew Losses 1942] by W R Chorley). The plane was lost over the North Sea on its way home as reported. Both Charlie and Ellis's names are together on the RAF war memorial stone at Runnymede. The details are as follows: He was in 35 Squadron, flying a Halifax II, W7760 TL-B and the operation was Hamburg. His fellow crew were: Sgt. P.H. Smith, Sgt. F.W. Huntley; Pilot Officer D.A. Holliger, Flight Sergeant N. McI Rattray (Royal Canadian Air Force), Sgt. E.A. Holland, Sgt. H.G. Le B. Pakenham-Walsh and Sgt. J.L. Graham. They took off at 2301 from Linton-on-Ouse. Last plotted in position 5447N 0600E and presumed lost over the sea.

Charlie is also mentioned as AC2 Charles Holland, being presumed drowned following the sinking of the SS Anselm on the 5th July 1941.

For many years, mother always lived in the hope that he might have been picked up and had somehow lost his memory. Mothers of course would always hope for a miracle, wouldn't they?

Time passed on, with just dad and myself carrying on the business, although by now he must have been feeling low. We were fortunate that dad's prudence with the paint and wallpaper materials had paid off. With just the two of us now, we were able to carry on looking after many of dad's old customers, without material shortages. Although at times we would have to improvise or make do with just one coat, where normally two or even three coats of paint would have been applied. During that time I learned a great deal from dad, what normally would have taken the full seven years apprenticeship had been concentrated into less than half the time and something I would be thankful for in later years.

Chapter Fourteen

A Taste of Victory

From the time of Dunkirk (May/June 1940) this was when the British Expeditionary Force was rescued from the beaches in France where the German Army had surrounded them. The rescue was made famous by the so-called 'little ships' crewed by civilians used in the evacuation that set of from the south coast. These little ships ranged from Mersey Ferries to private motorboats. The country had experienced only a feeling of dominance by the Germans and most of the time we'd had our backs to the wall. The RAF pilots with their Spitfires and Hurricanes had repelled the threat of invasion and with the moat of seawater surrounding us had saved us from the fate (occupation) that had befallen France, Belgium and Holland.

Yet these were only defensive victories, at least Dunkirk and the Battle of Britain had saved the day but then we were fighting alone. The offensive victory at El Alemein was a great victory in more ways than one. At last the jackboot (name given to German soldiers referring to their leather boots) had been booted out of Egypt and North Africa, it was a very heartening time for us all. The Germans weren't quite as invincible as they had thought.

One scene imprinted in my memory was that of a trainload of German Officers arriving at Windermere Station. Dad and I had gone to pick up Uncle Tom, dad's elder brother who was a retired railwayman. He was going to stay with us in the cottage for the week. We waited on the platform for the train to arrive, then when it did, we were astonished to see British soldiers get out first armed with pistols and rifles, then the prisoners of war (PoWs) followed on along the platform to the British Army transport that had been moved into the station exit. As they moved along, I stood there looking in amazement, their long grey green greatcoats, leather jackboots, peaked caps and brown tanned faces left me in no doubt from where they'd been captured. One in particular I couldn't take my eyes off, he was tall, slim, tanned and with his greatcoat draped over his shoulders. He reminded me so much of the film actor Conrad Viedt who used to often play the part of German officers in films. As he passed he saw me staring at him, I don't know what his thoughts were but his eyes and facial expression still conveyed a feeling of arrogance as he stared back!

Dad had left me when he saw that it was a prisoner of war train and had gone to enquire about the next train. Uncle Tom in the meanwhile came along from the guards van at the rear. Having been a railway official he was able to travel on any train with his lifetime pass. One couldn't mistake him, he had a big grey moustache, pot hat, with his watch and chain proudly fastened to his waistcoat. As we went outside the station we could see all the POWs climbing into the Army transport provided, then being whisked away to Grizedale Hall where they would be held. Amongst the more infamous German prisoners was Franz Von Werra, who became known as 'the one that got away!' He was the only German prisoner of war to escape back to Germany in World War Two. He made an unsuccessful attempt whilst at Grizedale and as a result he was moved to Canada, where he ultimately escaped back to Germany.

Later in 1943 one of my pals and I decided to cycle up to the Lake District for the September holidays. Dad said we could spend the week in the chalet by the lake, so we had prepared our bicycles well, and all our gear for the trip. We were now seventeen years old and knew that in the following year we would be conscripted into the Forces. One of my pals, Jackie Haydock, had already joined the Merchant Navy when he was sixteen and later was to lose the lower half of his leg in an incident at sea. Ronnie and Geoff, two more pals eventually went into the Navy, whilst Roy who was making the trip to the Lake District with me ended up in the RAF. This was probably the last holiday we would have out of uniform, so we would try to make the most of it.

We had only five more full days left until the Saturday before setting off in the early morning to the Lakes, when a knock came at the door. It was Arthur's father, one of Cec's pals. He was wanting to know whether Cec was home on leave, but Cec had been home a couple of weeks before from the Army and it would be a long time before he had another one. Frank, Cec and Arthur's other pal, had also been home on leave and gone back to the Navy. Arthur's dad seemed a bit worried so we invited him in. He told us that Arthur was coming home on sick leave after being in hospital for a month, and when he and his wife had visited him, he had been very quiet and withdrawn. They feared he was going to have a nervous breakdown.

Arthur's commanding officer had told them that his Lancaster bomber had been returning from a mission over Germany, it had reached England but was unable to land at their destination because of fog and poor weather conditions. It had been circling around for ages; then had been diverted to another airbase. Conditions were no better and running short of fuel it was forced to make a landing but had overrun the landing strip and crash landed in a field. All the crew had been killed except for Arthur who had received burns and had been traumatized by the ordeal.

We listened to Arthur's dad, as he explained what had happened and how he had hoped that either Cec or Frank would be home on leave. They were going to the hospital the next day to pick their son up. Mother putting her own grief to one side, said she would like to go round and comfort Arthur's mother.

Then I said, 'Would Arthur like to join Roy and myself on our trip to the Lakes? I explained to him about our plans for the following week and he was quite taken up with the offer. He knew that we all used to join in together when playing football, or hockey or roller skates, and bicycle rides to Blackpool and Southport. Many times on rainy days we'd all played card games together, so although Cec and his pals were a little older than us, two or three years was neither here or there. Mother went along with Arthur's father who was now feeling less worried about his son, who was still not yet twenty.

I remember when he came around the following night, how quiet and pale he looked after his ordeal. He wasn't in uniform and all night he didn't mention a word about the incident, and we were mindful to avoid the issue. In fact he spoke very little. Arthur had always been a quiet reserved lad, but it was plain to see it had affected him greatly. The prospect of going on a cycling holiday to the Lakes had somewhat cheered him, if that is the correct word to use. The look on his face showed a spark of his old self, he'd cycled to the Lakes before with Cec and Frank, and stayed at the cottage on quite a few occasions. It perked him up a little and gave him something different to think about and get his bicycle ready for the journey.

Come the Saturday morning the three of us set off on our seventy odd mile journey to the cottage. Mother and dad would already be there with two friends, and taken some of our luggage and we would carry on to the chalet. The journey went well, not much traffic then, except for Army transport. We arrived at the cottage mid afternoon, mother had made tea for us, which was most welcome and dad and their friends had been picking blackberries and damsons for us.

After tea dad suggested we take the Winchester and try to get a rabbit or two, but he made a point of giving the gun to Arthur instead of me and also later the keys to the chalet. There was always a reason behind his thinking, he simply said, You're the eldest and in charge!

Arthur had used the gun on previous occasions so it wasn't long before we were walking back with three rabbits. Then after we'd repacked with the extra things we made our way down to the lake. When we arrived at the chalet, Mr Dawson the farmer had delivered milk, eggs and butter for us together with a message to call at the farmhouse when we needed more, and not to worry about paying for it. It had been already agreed that dad would attend to the bill. 'Good old dad!'

After sorting ourselves out we decided to go for a row on the lake. There would be plenty of time for fishing as the week went on. After all that pedalling it was great to lie there in the boat then take our turn at rowing. We stayed on the lake for quite a while just enjoying the quietness and the rippling of the oars as they dipped in and out of the water. One wouldn't have dreamt there was a war on. In those days it stayed lighter in the evening because of the double British summertime. The Government had introduced this in order to extend the working day, so that it stayed light until 11 o'clock at night.

Arthur was still very quiet but I think both Roy and I could detect some sign of interest in his behaviour although we did not know what he was thinking. Before he had been 'called-up' into the Air Force he had been training to be a chef at the Midland Hotel in Manchester, so Roy and I elected him to do the cooking whilst we saw to the washing up and all the other chores. I remember sitting down that night, or rather in the early hours, to a large helping of rabbit stew with all the trimmings, even dumplings. Then finishing them off with stewed damsons, blackberries and custard. Needless to say we did not get up too early that Sunday morning.

Both Roy and myself realized, that although Arthur was beginning to react with a shade more enthusiasm, he was not the Arthur we had known two or three years before. The day was spent in a leisurely way, rowing, fishing and playing cards. On the Monday we cycled round the lake and down to Newby Bridge. Then up the west side to Ambleside and back again through Windermere and Bowness, and although it was holiday time there was little or no traffic on the roads due to petrol rationing, so the going was easy.

After a supper of fish and chips, the fish we'd caught, and superbly dished up by Arthur. We would have a little trip on the lake before darkness fell, then a game of cards before climbing into our bunks for the night. It was in the early hours that I awakened and noticed that Arthur's bunk was empty. I got up quickly wondering where he'd gone. The frightening thought, that in the frame of mind he was in, he might easily have gone out in the boat and jumped overboard. Roy was 'out to the world', so I didn't waken him, instead I quickly put on a few clothes and hurried outside. I could make out a figure sitting in the boat by the waterside and the glow of a cigarette, what a relief! I walked over to the boat with the excuse that I couldn't sleep.

I still didn't like the thought of leaving him on his own so we talked, and talked, and talked, with me doing most of it about happier times before the war when we all used to gang up together playing games and going on cycling trips. We had been sitting there most of the night looking over the lake, and I was finding it hard to think of things to talk about, when in the distance we could hear the faint drone of bombers returning from a mission. Then as they got nearer, I remember thinking this will put the tin hat on it now! It was just about the worst thing that could have happened. But how wrong can you be! As they passed over a little further towards the lower half of the lake we could just make them out as they droned along between the clouds. It seemed to have a wakening effect on Arthur because he started to talk openly, telling me about how they had encountered bad weather conditions on their return to England. Then overshot the runway, he said all that he remembered after that was dragging himself away from the plane, grasping the tops of the potato plants then turning to see the plane, broken in two, explode and set on fire. I listened, as he mentioned how the rest of the crew had perished in the crash, all their names one by one, and asking why was he the only one to escape?' I couldn't answer that really, I just said, 'You just happened to be lucky Arthur, the others weren't quite as fortunate. You can't blame yourself, it's just the way things happen!' With that he put his head in his hands and let it all out. Then after a while he looked up and said, 'I don't know what you must think of me, you've lost two brothers and here I am feeling sorry for myself!'

Poor Arthur, he'd been bottling all this up inside and feeling guilty because he was the only one who had survived, but at least he'd got it out of his system and maybe now he would accept that it was a stroke of luck that he had survived.

The planes had all gone and the droning with them except for one straggler who we could hear in the distance, then as the noise got louder, Arthur said, 'He's having trouble with the engines, can you hear? He's probably been hit.' Yes, he was quite right the engine sound was uneven, but it carried on limping home and out of hearing. 'He'll make it' Arthur said, 'at least the weather's clear!'

As we walked back to the chalet I knew by his manner that he was now on the mend, Roy was still 'out to the world' as we made a hot cup of tea then went to bed. The last few hours had been very well spent, as the following days and weeks were to reveal.

Roy noticed an immediate change in Arthur without knowing what had happened and so did my parents when we called to see them later on through the week. The training and tension for almost two years plus the accident had been too much for Arthur to take, but thankfully he'd survived and was now on the road to recovery. When the week came to an end we reluctantly made our way back home, with a holiday none of us would forget.

Roy and me would carry on at work and most evenings would see Arthur just as we would have done in our younger days. His parents couldn't believe the difference in him after just one week, but he would have to return to active service again when his long sick leave was over. He still had another tour of operations to complete when he returned. Before Arthur returned to the RAF, Cec and Frank came home on leave together. It was nice seeing them all strolling down the street together 'The three Musketeers!' as we always called them. How could we lose the war now?'

Dad's trophy he received for being 1st in Class 14 in 1926 Blackpool Speed Trials

Chapter Fifteen

Dad's Racing Days

I mentioned earlier that dad, in his younger days, had been a very keen amateur racing motorcyclist for Sunbeam, although this was before I was born, and I always remember the dozens of trophies, medals and paraphernalia around the house. I have the three trophies that he won at the Blackpool Speed Trials, the tallest one for the best overall performance. Unfortunately, over the years, the location of the medals and many other valuable trophies seem to have disappeared into thin air. No one seems to know what happened to them but these I have restored. Dad never seemed to be proud to show them, the thrill of racing seemed to be more important.

Although I worked with dad quite a lot during the early war years, he never spoke about his racing days, but Teddy told me how dad had lost his right eye in an accident whilst racing at Cockerham Sands. Apparently Teddy used to help him at each meeting with the motorbikes and on this particular day he was doing well, having won all the races in his class he was keen to win the last one. Teddy explained that in those early days, every so often the oil had to be pumped into the engine manually by means of a knob and shaft mounted on the tank. The knob had come off and dad was pumping away quite unaware in the excitement of the race that the metal shaft had pierced his hand between the forefinger and thumb, then when he needed both hands to turn, his hand was pinned to the tank.

When he awoke in the Lancaster Royal Infirmary with his eye and left hand bandaged up, he asked could he go home but of course they said, 'No!' However, later that night he got up, went into the toilets, donned an oilskin coat and a pair of Wellington boots, opened the window and climbed down a soil pipe, then hitch-hiked it back to Radcliffe. I couldn't believe it! But when I asked mother she said it was so. 'Well, you know your dad, he had a business to run and he wouldn't let that stop him!' Teddy said, 'He didn't because there on the following Monday morning he was giving the workmen their instructions as usual – and it didn't stop him from racing afterwards either!'

At the age of seventeen, like all my brothers, I wanted a motorbike too, but there was a war on. Each week I would look in the Radcliffe Times to see if any second-hand ones were being advertised but, of course, using less petrol than cars, they were more sought after. But one Saturday a Sunbeam was advertised for £7 and when I showed it to dad he agreed to go and see it.

It was only about a quarter of a mile away so we walked round to enquire about it with dad saying, 'Well it can't be much good for £7!' A lady answered the door and invited us into the small front room. She told us that she lived alone with her son who had been killed at El Alamein and the motorbike had been her son's pride and joy. She showed us into the tiny kitchen where her son had carefully cleaned it, greased it and placed it on wooden supports before covering it over with a large brown felt cloth.

As she removed the cover, she broke down in tears. Dad and I looked at each other as if to say, yes, we know just how you feel. So we took her back into the front room still sobbing uncontrollably. Luckily the door opened and her sister who lived a few doors away walked in. She told us that 'she' had advertised the motorbike. It was too much of a reminder for her sister every day. The tyres had been deflated so I had to run back home for dad's foot pump. When I returned the lady, comforted by her sister, was feeling better so whilst I was inflating the tyres, dad was paying for the bike. He had given her two £5 notes, you know, the old ones like tabloid newspapers! I don't think the poor woman had ever handled such wealth by the look on her face. 'I haven't any change to give you,' she said. Even if she had dad wouldn't have taken it anyway. 'Don't worry about the change, it's worth every penny,' he told her. And even as we pushed it back home, I heard him mutter under his breath a few times, 'Poor woman, losing her only son!' I think it had rekindled some of his personal feelings.

When we got home I couldn't wait to de-grease it and try it out, dad was eyeing it up all over and telling me all about it. It was a 1927 model, with a flat tank and, according to dad, a very good model. But it was my first motorbike and I wasn't bothered what it was, as long as I could travel about on it.

Finally, it was ready; dad had fuelled it but was doubtful about it starting, so after looking to see if the coast was clear, we pushed it into the side street. Then he got on it and said, 'Give me a push down onto James Street (from Joseph Street) as hard as you can,' which I did. Suddenly, it backfired in a cloud of smoke and dad was off like the shot of a gun with smoke trailing behind him, like one of the Red Devils Flying Team!

It must have been almost half an hour before he returned and I was getting rather worried, after all, he was now fifty-six and hadn't ridden a motorbike for almost twenty years. But when he did return with his cap on back to front and tears in his eyes, not to mention a big smile on his face, I knew then he was quite taken with it. 'Well, what do you think? I said. 'Well, it's a good machine but far too powerful for you to start on.' I think it was about 600 cc, so that was that.

I learnt later that he had taken it up with him to the Lake District when I was overseas in the Forces and sold it to the landlord of the Hare and Hounds at Bowland Bridge and he used it to travel to the shipyards at Barrow where he did his war work. I've heard it mentioned that people could hear him from miles away as he shot up Gummers How, past the Strawberry Bank Inn, then over the tops and down through Newby Bridge on his way to work.

J.H. Cookson (Ernie Shepherd Jnr)

Ernie Shepherd, (Snr) ploughing at Broad Oak Farm, Crosthwaite in 1941

Chapter Sixteen

We'll Meet Again

I had been working with dad decorating the front room of Broad Oak Farm, near Crosthwaite in 1943, this was on the east side of the Winster Valley about four miles from our cottage. Ernie and Ivy Shepherd owned the farm and ran it with the help of their two sons, Alan the eldest and young Ernie, who I became quite friendly with. I would often stay at the farm during holiday times helping young Ernie with the various tasks he would have to perform.

Broad Oak was a very neat and tidy farm as was the farmhouse itself, where Ivy took much pride in its immaculate appearance, so it was always a pleasure to stay, especially so with Ivy's home cooking which was on a par with mum's.

When not performing the farm tasks young Ernie and I would go out to catch rabbits which were quite abundant in those days, usually we'd use ferrets to flush them out of their burrows, but I remember walking back from the shop in Bowland Bridge one day with young Ernie and his friend Geordie Clarke. Geordie had two dogs, a greyhound called 'Nip' and a black and white sheepdog called 'Jim'.

We made our way back not along the road but through the fields and meadows until we reached a cornfield. The corn was high and still. It was a lovely day, so quiet and peaceful, who would have known that the world was in turmoil, people killing and being killed, it was hard to understand in this peaceful valley.

The cornfield had a strip of short grass about twenty feet (6 metres) wide along the whole width of the field as we entered through the gate, no doubt to allow for turning or working space for the horses and machines when cutting the corn, Ernie nudged me and murmured – 'Just watch this!'

Geordie gave instructions to the sheepdog that had been waiting eagerly for the word to 'go' which it did immediately the word was given, jumping up onto the dry stone wall then making its way to the other end of the field. Then it stopped and looked our way, as if waiting for further instructions which Geordie either must have beckoned or whistled. It jumped down into the field and started to beat from one side to the other barking and jumping as it went along.

In the meantime Nip's head was continually turning from one side of the

Harvest at Broad Oak Farm – having a well-earned tea break – 'drinkin!'
Left to right: Ernie Shepherd (Jnr), Harry Dobson (adjoining farm), two young holidaymakers behind, Ivy Shepherd,
Geoff Harrison, Ernie Shepherd (Snr), Alan Shepherd and Ken Park

Joseph Hardman (Ernie Shepherd Jnr)

field to the other waiting for something to emerge. I thought how intelligent these dogs are and they are enjoying every minute too. Then as the sheepdog's head bobbed up and it barked a little more excitedly the greyhound tensed its muscles ready for action! Suddenly a rabbit bolted out of the corn to the right of us, and Nip the greyhound was off like a bullet, catching up with it in no time grabbing it around the neck and tossing it into the air. It was obviously dead as it reached the ground, no doubt from a broken neck. Then no sooner had the greyhound returned and dropped its catch at Geordie's feet, another rabbit bolted from the corn only to meet the same fate.

What a team Geordie and his two dogs were! I had never seen anything like this before, who needs guns and ferrets with a team like this, two dogs and a boy. Geordie mentioned that he'd got seven rabbits from the cornfield a couple of days before and all without a mark on them, which was quite important as both Ernie and Geordie would sell them to a Mr Seddon who had a small chain of family shops back in Radcliffe and Farnworth.

Ernie Seddon was an old friend of my father and mother, and had stayed at our cottage on occasions before the war, then buying himself a small cottage at Tarnside between Bowland Bridge and Crosthwaite. Mr Seddon would mix business with pleasure by visiting his cottage every couple of weeks then go round the farms to buy or barter whatever he could to supplement the goods in his shops, maybe eggs, butter, ham or bacon, (or rabbits for sixpence [3p] each) so not only were Ernie and Geordie protecting their dad's field crops, but also providing themselves with a bit of sport and profit into the bargain.

Anyone who has watched 'Dad's Army' and 'Jonesy the butcher' will realise that meat rationing was quite a joke in wartime, with its 'bags of mystery' sausages and tinned 'sirloin of spam', so a rabbit pie was considered a mouth watering feast for many people living in the towns.

Ernie Seddon, a widower throughout the war years, married into a well-known Crosthwaite family, the Wallings, where he lived in the village with his wife Betty until he passed away in the 1980s.

It was now 1944, 'the invasion' had begun and once again I was on holiday at Broad Oak Farm when we heard the news on the wireless. At that point I wasn't to know that my brother Cec would be part of it, at least it was the beginning of the end, especially when the troops had established a foothold in France and Belgium and started to advance in spite of fierce opposition. For us at home, we could only keep our fingers crossed and pray that all would go well. In the meantime of course life would go on as usual. I remember well on the Saturday morning, bringing all the sheep down from the fields to be dipped, with young Ernie and myself riding on the horses back, everything after that was a complete blank until I regained consciousness at eight o'clock the morning after in Kendal Hospital (Westmorland County – now an old folks home).

I was told later, that after milking on the Saturday afternoon, five of us, Ernie, Alan, myself, Geordie and Alan Pearson, another friend, had set off to Kendal on our push bikes to see a film. As we were descending the hill past the old quarry (Penningtons) into Kendal, the buckle of my raincoat which had been tied over the handlebars, had caught in the spokes of the front wheel the sudden stop had catapulted me into the air and over into the road beyond, where I landed on the back of my shoulder and head. I'm told that I'd got up and was walking about in a bit of a dream continually asking the same question – 'What happened?'

However the boys took me to the hospital which was luckily close by, where I was examined and x-rayed, then admitted for a two weeks stay suffering concussion and a broken clavicle (collar bone), no doubt very lucky not to sustain more serious injuries. When I finally came round at eight o'clock the next morning – the chap in the next bed said, 'Well thank God for that, you must have asked me a hundred times since you came in – 'What happened?'

But from noon on the Saturday until eight o'clock the next morning those missing twenty hours have failed to return. I must have been thrown quite a distance, for when I saw the pushbike later, the sudden stop had caused the frame to buckle and the front wheel was touching the back one.

The invasion now was making good progress and as I lay recovering in the hospital wondering how Cec was faring, the ward door opened and in he walked in uniform but his right arm was in a sling too! I couldn't believe my eyes. He just walked up to my bed and said, 'Snap! I came off my bike too!' Actually he was a despatch rider in Belgium and had been blown off his motorbike by a German mortar bomb. We both had a good laugh about our plight, it was so good to see him and to know he was safe. We joked about not being able to tickle the trout and rowing round in circles with one arm in a sling.

Dad was struggling on by himself for a few weeks before he managed to find himself a new apprentice to take my place. He needed to keep the business ticking over at least, and Dennis Bradbury the new apprentice helped to do just that. Sonny too was granted compassionate leave to help keep the business going when dad fell sick, so at least when it was all over, the men would be able to carry on where they had left off.

After I had recovered it was my turn to wear a uniform. I had originally been informed it was the RAF but was told that as the war was now in its final stages, only Army personnel were needed and so I was reselected for the Royal Armoured Corps (tanks). The modern training regiment at Barnard Castle was ideally situated and with a similar landscape to the Lake District, I felt quite at home there.

It was a very well designed Army Camp with spick and span barrack rooms surrounded by lawns. The level of training and discipline was of the highest standard, so the feeling of 'esprit-de-corps' was paramount throughout each squadron, cleanliness and smartness was very important. I remember one particular Friday evening, when I was waxing and polishing around my bedspread, as we all had to do for inspection the next morning and I saw a pair of very muddy boots standing in front of me, not even on the paper I was putting down to protect it. I was just about to blow my top when a voice said, 'I didn't know they were training you to be char lady!' I looked up quickly, I couldn't believe my eyes it was Cec with a big grin on his face. I asked him how he'd managed to get here, then with a nod to the window he said, 'You see that camp over the other side of the railway line, well I'm stationed in that first hut.' It was less than five hundred yards away, just over the other side of the single railway line to Broomilaw Station, so all he had to do was climb the fences and walk over.

When Cec had been given my address from home he couldn't believe it was the next camp to his and even more so, when he could see me through his binoculars, he said he'd been watching me come and go for most of the day. What a coincidence! We celebrated in the Naffi with egg and chips, although Cec had to pay, my weekly pay then was only ten shillings (50p) and it didn't stretch to such extravagances.

This was a great stroke of luck and we could spend Saturday evenings together and even travel home together occasionally on a weekend pass. Cec was only attached to the training regiment because of his temporary situation and seemed to be in a more flexible position than I was when it came to obtaining thirty-six or forty-eight hour passes. But eventually the training came to an end and coincided with VE Day. Now we would have to retrain, this time for the Far Eastern conflict, which was a completely different kind of warfare. This took another three months. We had been on manoeuvres for the last few weeks in Durham and Yorkshire and on the last day of training, halted outside our base at Barnard Castle. The idea was to clean all our equipment then make our return smartly back into Camp. We had just about finished our chores and had our tea when I got in the tank and put on the headphones to listen in to the six o'clock news. The news was sensational the war was as good as over. A new type of bomb, the

Atomic Bomb, had been dropped on Hiroshima in Japan and completely demolished the city, then another was dropped in Nagasaki and within a few days the war was expected to be over.

I climbed onto the turret and shouted the news to the rest of the crew. They didn't believe me at first and it was only when they put their own earphones on and heard it, did it sink in. The whole squadron was cheering it was tremendous.

So on the final day of retraining, the war had at last come to an end. I was thirteen when it started and nineteen when it ended. It would be another two years before I was back in civilian life. In the meantime, all the longest serving men would be demobbed first and we would have to take their places. Our regiment was sent to the Middle East and we were distributed to different places to release the men who hadn't seen their families for years.

Me and five others ended up in the Headquarters Cairo District, Kasr-El-Nil Barracks, situated right on the side of the Nile in Cairo itself. We soon learned the work we'd been assigned to do in the various branches there, although it was quite different from our tank training days and I enjoyed my time there. My responsibility was to take care of all official and private mail and also print out the area orders etc on a Gestetner printing machine. The war was over and we considered ourselves very fortunate that we would not have to endure the long days of hardship, suffered by the men who were at last heading home. The look on their faces 'said it all!'

Our Christmas menu in 1946 was one to be remembered, after six years of wary, we'd almost forgotten what real food tasted like. One of my pals in A' Branch typed out the menu on a wax typing sheet, whilst I painstakingly scratched out the design with a pin. The menu started of with breakfast, traditional Christmas dinner right through to tea and supper in the evening. It was lovely! Sadly we evacuated from Cairo soon after in the summer of 1947.

Me and three pals (Bill and Billy O'Neil) at Kasr-El-Nil Barracks taken on Gezira Island. Headquarters can just be seen in the background

Chapter Seventeen

Back to the old routine

Returning home again on the troop ship was a very nice feeling, even though my stay in Cairo was an experience to be remembered, all the history, pyramids, bazaars, people and way of life. So different from ours, it had been quite an education in itself and in our free time we took the opportunity to visit as many places of historic interest that we could.

We disembarked at Liverpool and had two weeks leave. We would have to spend a little time still before our release came so it was tank training again, but whatever for I shall never know. We might as well have been released there and then and allowed to go home to help restore all the properties that had been neglected over six years of war.

I was now attached to the Second Royal Tank Regiment and we were sent to Germany, to retrain, but apparently the three squadrons over there couldn't accommodate another Lance Corporal, so I had to make my own way to C' Squadron, at Warminster. As I travelled back on the train through Germany I was completely stunned by the amount of devastation in the towns and cities. It reminded me of the time when Manchester was bombed, but this was on a far bigger scale.

Once back in England it was just a matter of waiting my turn to be demobbed. All I wanted to do now was carry on where I'd left off, although this time all the men would be back out of uniform, with many tales to tell of their experiences. The day finally arrived (1st week in January 1948) and I received my £60 gratuity payment, demob suit for services rendered and a form that allowed me to claim a full driving licence. I was also given the

Dennis and myself in 1957 in Cockle Park, Radcliffe – I lived on Spring Lane (2nd house on the left and Catholic Church on right)

95

choice of claiming one for the two provisional licences I held during wartime, as they didn't have driving tests then. Thus accepting that having held two provisional licences I would be competent enough to drive a car anyway.

By the end of 1947 mother and dad had moved out of the family house and would soon be living at the cottage. It had been a cruel war for them, so the peaceful environment of the countryside would help to ease the bad memories of war and the grief it had brought and maybe help to recall the good times we had all enjoyed in the 1930s.

Sonny, our eldest brother, was now running dad's business with the help of Cec and the workmen, who had all returned safely, so when I rejoined the firm, things were bustling again. It was indeed a very busy time and of course now, wallpaper and paint materials were all much easier to obtain. I carried on looking after the creative side of the business, doing the kind of work dad and I used to do. I redecorated many of the houses where Ellis had worked before the war, so the inspiration for creative décor would live on, in just the same way. Of course creative décor then, always required a helping hand, for many reasons, rollers and emulsion paint which make the work faster and easier these days had not yet been invented, so when a ceiling or large wall area required painting or patterning two hands were always better than one, providing of course each person worked in unison.

Dennis had taken over as dad's apprentice when I left to join the Forces, so the routine that dad had taught us both blended together very well, just as Ellis and Syd's working partnership had done before the war. Dennis and I would carry on with all the decorative work in the business and there was much of it to do after six years of wartime 'make do and mend'.

By 1950 acrylic and emulsion paint was now beginning to replace the old oil bound water paints and distempers, these new paints would be useful also for reducing the amount of time required when painting on the background coats for the wall effects. So they were a great benefit to the specialist decorator, as was the paint roller when introduced later.

However the semi-transparent beeswax glaze we always used then to colour and finish the wall effects could not be substituted very successfully with emulsion or acrylic mixtures. In fact, even up to date I have not yet discovered any other finishing glaze to compete with this natural ingredient, which is why, during the 1960s when beeswax glaze was discontinued in favour of a substitute ingredient, I decided I would have to try and make my own, which eventually I did to my great satisfaction.

Those early post war years held many amusing memories for all the men who returned to their jobs after serving in the various branches of the Forces. Many times we would all work together on large buildings. On one such occasion when the weather was quite atrocious, all those who had been working on exterior painting jobs, were sent to help with the interior of a very large empty house in Whitefield, just a short distance away where Teddy and one or two others were working.

Teddy would find them all different jobs to keep them busy for the day, but of course there was a shortage of steps and planks to go round. Eventually everyone was sorted out and given jobs to do. We didn't have transistor wireless sets in those days but nevertheless the air would be filled with the sound of music coming from different rooms. I suppose everyone had something to sing about then after being away from home so long and the competition coming from different parts of the house would get quite intense.

The renderings would range from the popular songs of the day to Teddy's version of 'Bless this House' with his own words to the verses, some of which I remember well:

'Bless these windows painted white
Letting in large lumps of light and
Bless these chimneys long and tall
Belching black smoke over all.'

I also remember on one job before he was called into the Army he ended one verse with:

'Bless these doors so firm and stout
Keeping Charlie Holland out!'

At that minute dad walked in through the front door, he just smiled and put his finger to his lips, he walked out and came in again this time slamming the door behind so Teddy would hear. Dad knew it was just meant in jest as they all got on well together and respected one another. Whilst working on a particular job in the large house, the singing was interrupted when Johnny who had been painting round the kitchen window shouted 'man overboard!' Stan came hurtling down from the bathroom window above, with a loud trailing shout. Luckily a bush had broken his fall and apart from being drenched in soap and water he had escaped unhurt.

Of course when everyone knew he wasn't hurt Stan came in for a great deal of ribbing. The bathroom Stan and the apprentice had been working on had a blue ceiling and a white cloud effect painted on the walls above the tiled dado, with anaglypta seagulls and a crested wave border around the base for effect. Ellis had done this work before the war so now Stan was washing it down and at the same time singing, 'I'm painting the clouds with sunshine!'

It had been a little unfortunate for Stan that the plank he and the apprentice had been working on was a bit too long. He had opened the two tall windows and put a small box in the window bottom, with the plank protruding through, Stan was standing on the end when the apprentice at the other end climbed onto the steps and took his weight off, Stan went see sawing out of the window!

All through the lunch break Stan had to endure jokes like, 'It's a good job you fell on a very hardy laurel bush! Don't put too much soap on the clouds next time!' Johnny who'd been working in the kitchen below said, 'Well I've been in the Navy for five years and it's the first time I've seen anybody walk the plank!' Stan took it all quite seriously, maintaining that if he hadn't learned the correct way to fall whilst he'd been in the Ancillary Fire Service (AFS), fighting fires in the London blitz, then he could have been carried home in a box! Then what would you have done? I don't remember whom it was that said, 'We'd have had a whip round for a Union Jack then slipped you down the plank through the window!'

All this of course was in good clean fun I think the men were just so happy to be back home again, they just let themselves go whenever the opportunity came along. They were very enjoyable years.

Chapter Eighteen

Hangman!

During the early 1950s Dennis and myself went to help on a job in Farnworth about four miles away, at a large public house called the 'Rawsons Arms'. The landlord was the then assistant hangman, Harry B. Allen. Dennis and I had visions of a sombre looking person walking round like 'the man in black!' When we arrived and walked through into the bar area and saw a notice pinned above saying 'No hanging around the bar' and then a smiling face wishing us good morning, we were quite relieved to say the least.

It was quite a large awkward staircase that had to be decorated and it required quite a few pairs of hands each day to sheet up, scaffold, and then paint. One morning we were all awaiting the arrival of the 'Hangman' himself, Mr Pierpoint. They were setting off to perform an execution in London. Harry had told us when Pierpoint arrived to let him know that he was ready upstairs, and to go up the backstairs if he wanted to.

None of us had ever seen or met him but we hinted 'in front of the apprentice', that he was a Frankenstein figure like Boris Karloff (born William Henry Pratt). So naturally by the time the knock sounded on the front door the apprentice's knees were knocking together like a pair of drumsticks, but he managed to pluck up enough courage to open the door and was confronted by a tiny figure, smaller than him. It was Mr Pierpoint the Hangman. The apprentice was trying to explain to him that the pub wasn't open yet, not realizing it was Mr Pierpoint but when he explained who he was, he came hurrying in to the foot of the stairs, which of course was blocked.

We were all surprised when we saw him, not a bit like one would imagine a hangman to be. We passed on the message we had been given, he said he wouldn't go up as he was in a hurry and they had a long way to travel. We'd shouted up to Harry to say he'd arrived, but the little man below was impatiently marching backwards and forwards. Then he came to the foot of the stairs again and shouted up, 'Come on Harry, don't keep me hanging about down here!' We had been quietly working away on the scaffold and on hearing that it sparked off, first a giggle, then it turned into a kind of stifled laughter, which made him realize the other meaning of what he'd said and he turned away a little embarrassed. We were relieved to hear a voice shouting down, 'Right Albert I'm ready!'

Sylvia and me on our wedding day

T. Barlow, Bury

We asked Harry if he thought that capital punishment was a deterrent to murder? As just at that time the subject of abolition was in the newspapers. He said, 'That although he thought it would never be a complete deterrent, the thought of paying for your crime in this way, would deter nine out of ten people who would contemplate murder, but the tenth would always think they could get away with it and do it regardless.' Harry also added, that if capital punishment was ever abolished, then, in his opinion murders would become ten a penny! As they now have! The last executions took place in 1964, at Walton, Liverpool and Strangeways, Manchester. In December 1969 Parliament confirmed the abolition of capital punishment for murder and in 1999 it was totally abolished.

I suppose there must have been many more amusing times during those early years after the war. I remember one in particular was when I went to help Teddy and an apprentice complete his job on the last day. Teddy showed me the rooms he had done (which of course as always, were first class) and the rest work to be completed that day. So we then got on with the rest of the work in hand. Then at lunchtime when we had more time to talk, he mentioned about the bathroom he'd been finishing off the day before. In those days many bathrooms and kitchens would have a painted dado then finished off with a line around the top. Teddy had been completing the line using a straight edge and lining fitch (specialist brush) when the lady of the house brought him a cup of tea and tapped on the door.

The bathroom was a little lower than the landing level, so when she opened the door and looked at the wall from above, the line didn't appear to be quite straight. This was caused by a slight bulge in the wall surface, once in the bathroom and viewing it head on, the line was perfectly straight. She stood there with the cup of tea in her hand, she said, 'Oh Teddy! I don't think the lines quite straight.' Teddy having his little joke, just said, 'Well that's because it's still wet, when its dry, it will pull out straight!' I smiled as he told me and even more so when he said that she'd mentioned to him that he was right about the line, it had gone straighter now it was dry. 'You should have waited for me to put the line on Teddy,' I said, 'I've had a lot of practise painting lines on curved surfaces. Teddy looked at me, 'Oh, when was that?'

His eyes nearly popped out of his head when I told him, I said, 'Well as you know during the war the girls couldn't buy silk stockings, so Jean and Audrey would ask me to go into the workshop for powder colours to tint their legs with. They'd mix the shades on a saucer, then sponge it onto their legs to imitate the stocking colour. 'Well!' said Teddy with eyes and ears agog. 'Well as you also know,' I said, 'they used to have a seam running down the back and so to complete the effect I always had to paint them on because they could never get them straight.' Teddy turned to the apprentice and jokingly told him, 'Not to listen, he wasn't old enough!' Then went onto say, 'How come you always got the best jobs, when all I get to do are bathroom walls?' 'How did you manage to keep a steady hand?' Teddy asked. I said, 'Well, when they're your sisters you don't think anything about it, but after that Jean would bring one of her friends for the same treatment when they were getting ready to go dancing, she was a very good looking girl, with a shapely figure similar to Jean's!' 'Well go on!' said Teddy impatiently. I said, 'Well, it wasn't easy to keep a steady hand whilst she was standing on the chair, and the first time I tried, it looked like a snake crawling up the back of her leg.' Then Teddy said with his usual wit, 'You should have painted a ladder on the other one!' 'Why I asked?' 'Well she might have let you play a few games with her!' he quipped. The lady of the house must have wondered what the joke was with all the loud laughter going on especially when he added, 'Well I've never heard of a job before where you start at the bottom and work your way down!'

Teddy was like this all the time so as you can imagine anyone who worked with him was always in for a good laugh and any apprentice whom he taught was very fortunate to receive his excellent tuition.

I went round to see my sister Evelyn at her hairdresser's shop and she had this lovely young girl, Sylvia Downs working for her. We started going out together and a few years later we were married on 22nd September 1951 at Ringley Parish Church, between Farnworth and Radcliffe. Our first house was at 364 Bolton Road, Radcliffe.

As the years went on however it was obvious that times were changing, the long rows of houses we once used to paint as one unit were now becoming individually owned, and new laws required inside toilets, bathrooms and better kitchen facilities etc. So landlords were now selling them to the tenants who were eligible for grants to help with these improvements. This meant of course that there were more opportunities open for the young tradesmen to start up their own businesses, and so it was inevitable that many of the young men who had returned from the war would grasp the opportunity to work for themselves now that home ownership was becoming popular, whether they be plumbers, electricians, builders, plasterers or decorators.

Arnold and George, two of dad's eldest workmen before the war decided to branch out on their own. Smaller businesses were now the order of the day and of course they had all learned their jobs well. I remember Jack, my wife's cousin, handing his notice in one day. Jack had been in the Marines and had returned to complete his decorating apprenticeship, and was very interested in wood graining and marbling techniques. He had attended night school classes at Bolton regularly and now he had qualified as a teacher in the arts, so we were all pleased with his achievement. Jack carried on teaching until retirement, mostly in Ireland, but decided to return to his hometown, his health wasn't very good at all.

My wife and I visited Jack and his wife Moira some eighteen months before he passed away, and I was quite surprised when he gave me all his prized expensive equipment, tools and brushes used to create the various effects. He could no longer use them himself and said he just wanted them to be looked after and used for the work as intended. It was a much-appreciated gesture as many similar brushes and tools of mine were very worn, and so I took them gratefully as a compliment, he wouldn't accept a penny for them.

Chapter Nineteen

Moving on – Canada!

During the 1950s things were only just returning to normal, some rationing was still in effect and many items were still not easy to obtain, but certainly everything was getting much easier as time went on. I remember the sweet ration had been doubled from six ounces (175 g) to twelve ounces (350 g), and then abolished altogether when Mr Churchill was made Prime Minister again, as were many items. Petrol was easier to obtain, although I do remember we had to use red petrol for commercial purposes and white for pleasure, which sometimes could be a little frustrating.

It had been a long war and left many scars in the lives of many people, just as it had done in my family, it could never be quite the same again for those who had lost husbands and sons, and even those who had made it back home after seeing the carnage in battle, or surviving the prisoner of war camps in Europe and the Far East, they must have had some very hard times indeed.

By now most had returned, and had picked up the threads where they had left off, and as far as work was concerned there certainly was no shortage. Everywhere was thriving, making up for the lost years, people buying their own houses for as little as £300, which is what I paid for my first house, although it wasn't in very good condition at the time. Probably the average house price would have been a little more in better condition.

Proudly standing outside our first house with Gillian our baby daughter in 1953

Travelling to the Lake District to visit my parents with my wife and baby daughter Gillian, born in 1953, posed very little problem, they were now settled in the cottage at Hartbarrow surrounded by green fields and trees, although it was still quite basic and with no electricity. Dad had by now fitted Calor gas lights and installed a bathroom and inside toilet. Mother had her lovely garden and her favourite colour was yellow, she loved the daffodils in the spring and the yellow brooms.

Dad had moved the little wooden chalet from Blakeholme and erected it in the field above the cottage. He had added a lounge, a small kitchen and toilet and it was used for the family when staying overnight. The view over the Winster Valley was quite fantastic, although it was unfortunate that it had to be removed from the Lakeside, as the site was to be taken over for commercial purposes. Its new location, at least, was now more convenient for visiting purposes.

Mother and dad went to Canada around this time to visit relatives and that gave me the idea to emigrate. Post war England was quite austere compared with the lure of the wide-open spaces of Australia, New Zealand and Canada and as there was assisted passage to these countries at the time this was an added incentive. The urge to travel and start a new life in Canada attracted me, as it did many others at that time. The actual cost was only £10.

We sold our home, which was now in excellent order, for £1,200 (four times the initial price). The plan was for me to travel over alone and when I'd got a job and a house, Sylvia and Gillian would follow on. Meanwhile they would stay with her parents in a tavern near Farnworth. At this time flying was not as popular and I made the journey over on the 'Empress of France' embarking from Liverpool.

The journey on the ship took about seven days and was quite enjoyable, excellent food and service and was full of young men and couples looking for a new life in Canada. I shared a cabin with three other young men all with the same objective in mind. We had much in common, which of course helps when you're parted from family. Although we eventually went our own ways, during my stay I happened to meet each one by accident at later times and places.

Arriving in Canada and travelling down the St. Lawrence River was a wonderful experience. Seeing all the different roof colours on the houses as we travelled down, Quebec first, where we disembarked for a short stay, then on to Montreal my destination, where I was to meet Frank, one of our apprentices who had returned after serving in the Navy.

Frank had married a Canadian girl who he'd met when in the Forces, they had lived in Gig Lane, Bury, facing the football stadium, but decided to live in Canada. We'd kept in touch, and he found me a job. Frank was waiting and shouted to me in a warm Canadian accent 'Hi there!

I stayed with Frank and his wife for about six weeks but wasn't too keen on the place of work, they all spoke French and the type of work wasn't exactly my cup of tea. So I decided to move on to where I could at least understand what people were saying.

I made the trip down to Hamilton in Ontario where mum and dad's friends lived and found a job there. This was an improvement although the work again was not what I was looking for but at least I had the opportunity to visit mum and dad's relatives who lived on a farm some fifteen miles out of town. This made me feel a little more at home and was somewhere to go to at weekends. As time went on I realised that the type of work I was seeking would not be forthcoming, ordinary painting work seemed to be the only option, and of course DIY (Do it yourself) was further advanced here than in England at this time. I then took a job working for the Board of Education as a joiner, which was more interesting to me than plain painting.

It was then I decided to return home and start again, so after spending nearly twelve months in Canada I returned home again on the same ship, but with mixed feelings. I liked many things about the country, everything was on a far larger scale than England but what one views on postcards and brochures isn't always what it seems! The trip home was quieter, although I did meet others who had experienced much the same thing as I had, but at least I had learned quite a lot which would be useful in later years, and I had also seen another wonder of the world – Niagara Falls!

Chapter Twenty

Chalet Home

It was good to be home, and to see all the family again, now we would have to make a fresh start, Cec was waiting for me when we arrived in Liverpool, with Sylvia and Gillian, who was by now just three years old. She must have wondered who this strange person was and where I'd appeared from but of course as time moves on, life returns to normality and it wasn't long before we had settled in another home and started our lives together again.

In 1962 mother passed away in hospital, with cancer. Dad was now on his own so Sylvia and I decided to move house and live in the little chalet above the cottage we moved there in September 1964. Cec and his two boys had been living with mother and dad after his marriage had broken up in 1959 but he was now planning to remarry and move nearer to Kendal. Dad was lost without mother, so at least we could look after him and it was a good opportunity to build our own bungalow, which we had always wanted to do and as far as work was concerned I would be working with Cec again. Sylvia had sold her hairdressing shop 'The Beauty Spot' which she ran with her partner, my sister Evelyn.

In 1965 our son Stuart was born. The chalet was now getting a little cramped so I extended it temporarily, adding a bathroom and larger kitchen until the permission to build the bungalow was finally granted. I was going to build around and over it, whilst still living in it. Quite a task, but in fact the idea worked very well, I was able to start work on it in the mid 1970s.

Our chalet home set in beautiful surroundings in 1946-47

Gillian aged 10, outside the Bowland Bridge shop

Dad with his red and cream two-tone van at Strawberry Bank
with Whitbarrow in the distance

Ian Davenport

When Cec remarried and moved away from the cottage my sister Evelyn came in 1965 to live with dad. She had lost her husband Sydney, who had been in the Coldstream Guards during the war. At least now, dad had plenty of hands to take care of him.

Stuart our son, started school in 1969, at the small school on the fell, by the side of St Anthony's Church, where mother and later dad were buried. He was the last pupil to be admitted to the school before it was closed in 1971, almost one hundred years after it had first opened. It only had one teacher, Mrs Morrison, and less than a dozen pupils of mixed ages up to eleven. It must have been quite a task trying to keep them occupied, whilst teaching the different age groups various subjects.

St Anthony's, Cartmel Fell   John Marsh Archive

I was working with Cec one day, when I received a telephone message from Sylvia to say that Stuart and an older boy had gone missing from school. There was a big search involving the police. Cec and I jumped in the car and drove home as quickly as we could to find everyone in a state of panic. They had been missing since morning break and now it was well into the afternoon and there was still no sign of them. Local people were searching the woods and fields around the school and terrible thoughts were going through my mind, maybe they'd been picked up by a car, or drowned in a pond?

It was a cold and icy November day and soon the light would be fading. The police dogs hadn't found a trace of them and a helicopter had been alerted to search the area before darkness fell. There was a tarn on the fell above the school and I made my way up the hillside as quickly as I could, fearing the worst. When I arrived gasping for breath, I could see the tarn was still frozen over. Maybe they'd been playing on it and fallen through the ice, all these things ran through my mind. After a quick search around I couldn't find any footprints or broken ice to my relief, so I made my way back to the schoolhouse.

As I arrived back I could see the police dogs being put back into the van and a police officer on the radio reporting that the two boys had just been found safe and well. I ran into the schoolhouse and I could see everyone crowding around a small-bewildered figure sitting down at the table, with his school dinner in front of him. The dinner van had stayed on with it being the last call, which as it happened had been just as well.

My wife and Mrs Morrison explained what had happened. The older boy had apparently enticed Stuart to wander off to his house about a mile away. Stuart couldn't tell us much about it except that they were wandering around in the fields and woods and he became lost and frightened. However a farmer travelling up the road to Hodge Hill near the school found him wandering along the road, not knowing where he was going, the farmer being aware that a search was going on brought Stuart back to school much to everyone's relief!

Dad sadly died in 1970 aged eighty-three – he had a good life and was dearly loved by all his family.

Chapter Twenty-one

Fish and Chips please!

Whilst waiting for planning permission to build our bungalow I had been transforming the land around and in front of the wooden chalet. It was just a sloping field with a small stream running down it. I would spend much of my spare time digging paths all the way round to terrace the slopes, planting shrubs and trees, building retaining walls, septic tanks and finishing the landscaping first, as I knew that when I had to start the bungalow proper, I probably wouldn't have much time for anything else, or at least that was what I thought.

Dad with Bert and Edith Lever and their nephew David when they took over the village shop in Bowland Bridge in the late 1960s   Ian Davenport

Both Cec and I worked separately in our decorating businesses, but helped each other whenever either of us required a helping hand. We had been working together for quite a large industrial concern that had just closed down. So we carried on doing our own thing for a month or two. It was then that I decided to have a break from decorating and go into business in Kendal, and bought a fish and chip shop, in Stramongate, that seemed to have lots of potential. The business was owned by Mr and Mrs Wilson, an elderly couple and was seldom open. They had many people wanting to purchase the business but because they couldn't show a steady turnover they couldn't get the asking price. To me it seemed well worth it considering its position and the lack of competition in the vicinity. I went back to the chalet that evening and said to my wife and daughter, 'How would you like a fish and chip shop in Kendal?' Happily they took the idea 'with a pinch of salt' and didn't believe me until I said, 'Alright, I'll take you to see it!' Only then would they believe me, and it was something quite 'out of the blue'.

I'm sure this was one of my better decisions as the shop turned out to be far busier than even I had anticipated. It was hard work especially at the start when we'd both gone in at the deep end. I hadn't a clue how to fry fish and chips, but 'practise makes perfect!' Both Sylvia and Gillian quickly got into the routine and soon we were able to employ extra staff to help out, which we certainly needed. It was called 'Holland's Fish and Chip Shop'.

My staff in March 1981. From the left: Eva Bingham, Mary Mattison, Pat Gregg, me and Sylvia, Millie Gould and Ann Sill

Kendal in the 1970s was a bustling town with always something going on for all ages, with its picture houses, bingo hall, shows at the old Brewery Arts Centre and seasonal functions like, the Torchlight Procession usually held on a Friday evening in September. This was followed the next day by the 'Push up the River' involving races in kayaks and canoes etc against the flow of the River Kent, which happened to run under Stramongate Bridge alongside our shop.

Then on the Saturday evening we would be inundated with spectators and participants of the Harness Racing Club or 'Horse Trotters' as we would always call them. These were very busy times as you can imagine and seldom would Sylvia and I get home before three or four o'clock on the Sunday morning, as the shop always had to be clean and tidy ready for the next session.

All these activities provided the shop with busy evening trading sessions as did the local businesses during lunch time sessions. Kendal Socks (now a modern office building) just around the back of the shop, which now all seem to be made in Taiwan and the thriving K Shoes which now sadly seems to be non-existent. The large Provincial Insurance Headquarters immediately facing our shop (now flats) with many other small businesses phoning in orders, not to mention the droves of schoolboys who would invade us at noon, for sausage and chips and steak puddings with it's 'special' gravy mix!

Providing quick lunches in a short space of time required good efficient staff who knew exactly what they were doing and ours certainly did. We all enjoyed working together so much so that I was able to retain the same girls throughout the 1970s. This made the task of working and running the shop so much easier with not actually living on the premises ourselves, although our daughter Gillian and her husband David did, for a short spell, when they married in 1975. There was adequate space above the shop that David made into quite comfortable living accommodation.

I suppose in many shops with late night opening sessions it pays to have a good understanding with the officers on the beat (police) as there are occasions when cooperation is appreciated by both. I remember three occasions very well, once when a large group of Manchester United Supporters arrived back in town a little the worse for drink and went on the rampage. A blue helmet popped through the door and advised us to close early, which we promptly did, and a good job too. Soon after, the road in front of the shop was swarming with shouting and fighting fans, some annoyed and drunk, possibly their team had lost, but whatever the reason it was just mayhem outside. It reminded me of the 'Keystone Cops' – chasing red striped fans in all directions, over Stramongate Bridge and the Provincial car park. The Police then bundling them into the awaiting 'Black Maria's', eventually most of them had dispersed except for a few more persistent and aggressive fans, who had bunched themselves around the front entrance of the Provincial offices. They weren't about to move without a struggle it was plain to see, that was until the dog handler arrived with a couple of well trained Alsatians, just a little dash towards them with bared teeth and they were herded into the Black Maria like a 'flock of lambs!'

The second occasion was something most of the town most dreaded when hordes of scooters would invade us like a swarm of locusts. It was quite intimidating when the 'scooter brigade' descended on the town. I remember on one occasion there had been an incident in the Chinese Take Away owned by Mr Yeung (sadly died at 50 years old), a little further up the street where a knife had been used. As I walked into the shop from the kitchen I could see that Mary, one of my assistants was having trouble with two unsavoury looking characters that were refusing to pay for their supper. I thought it best not to press them under the circumstances, with the knife still being sought but a third young man who was paying for his order at the end of the shop, suddenly put his hand in his pocket and produced his police warrant card and said, 'You had better pay up before I take you to the Station!' We were surprised but pleased to find out he was an off duty policeman, which was more than the other two customers were. I believe the knife was found later although I'm not sure whether the culprit was ever identified.

The third incident happened one Saturday night when we'd finished the week's sessions, cleaned and locked up the shop and walked over to our cars on the Provincial car park opposite, one of my assistants Millie had loaned me her car as mine was in the garage for body repair. Her car was an old Austin Maxi and the driver's door wouldn't lock. As I opened it I noticed a strong fruity smell, but not being my own car I ignored it, throwing my coat over the back seat in the dark and my leather bag with the week's takings on the passenger seat. Sylvia was not with me that night.

The three assistants in the other car moved off with me following on, then as we approached the traffic lights at the top of Lowther Street, I instinctively felt over into the back seat, 'my hand touched what appeared to be a body.' I froze for a few seconds, wondering whether it was a dead body or whether someone was waiting for me to reach a lonely road out of town, knock me on the head and make off with the takings. There was no sound at all from the back seat, so it could be either.

The traffic lights changed to green and the assistant's car turned to the right – all hands waving within, I was supposed to carry straight on, so when I turned right alongside them which I had never done before they must have wondered why I had done so but I didn't want to wind the window down and shout to them in case the person in the back was purposely being quiet. When we reached the end of the main street they turned right again whilst I carried straight on with a parting wave. So they went round the one-way system to their homes, probably still wondering why I had changed my routine.

I arrived at the Police Station and quickly got out and ran into the Station and told them. Six policemen ran out and surrounded the car. Two opened the back doors and pulled the body out before jumping astride, which wasn't for long as it reeked of booze and was out to the world. It turned out to be one of the local wino's who had been taken in earlier, then released. So that was that!

It was always reassuring to know that on dark winter nights one could rely on help or assistance whenever it was needed, in the same way that a hot drink or fish and chips in the back kitchen would be appreciated!

Work in progress on our bungalow. Me and my son-in-law David in 1973-74

These years were very busy indeed, it was a case of rushing into Kendal to work in the shop, then rushing back again to work on the bungalow and then back again to reopen for the evening session. It wasn't without its humorous incidents like the day when I'd got to the point of removing part of the wooden chalet roof to make way for a supporting beam. It was Wednesday and I only had the lunch time session to do that day, so I had covered the opening with a large piece of thick polythene

Close up of the Chalet in the early 1950s, with Edith Lever, her mother and daughter Wendy. They stayed here while waiting to take over the shop in Bowland Bridge.

Our lovely bungalow finished at last! High Hartbarrow in 1986

Cec, myself and Dennis in the late 1990s – decorating a house by the shores of Windermere

sheeting until I returned from Kendal after completing the lunch session. Sylvia was staying at home that day anyway, so everything was going fine. I'd been wondering how to get over this little problem and planned it for my half day off. But like all plans they seldom go as smoothly as one would like them to. I was busy frying away, when Sylvia phoned to say it was raining quite heavily and the polythene was beginning to 'belly down' in the middle. She had been trying to lift it up with the sweeping brush, but it was coming down so hard it wasn't working. There was not a drop of rain in Kendal and it had been quite a nice day when I'd left home.

I told her to make a small hole in the polythene and put a bin underneath it as it was over the kitchen she would be able to bale it out and put it into the washbasin. I'd almost finished the session anyway, so it wasn't long before I was on my way. Then as I climbed out of Kendal and started to descend down the other side of Underbarrow Scar, I could see how black the sky was over the Cartmel Fell range, then through Crosthwaite and it was coming down in torrents. When I finally reached, home, the bubble had burst in spite of all her efforts and the kitchen looked like a children's paddling pool!

In spite of everything the building work progressed very well and I managed to dig out and complete the foundations in the early spring. I erected all the outer walls and roof framework by August but of course before the roof could be slated, I had to remove the wooden chalet and build the supporting inner walls. This would be a little awkward as we were trying to live in it at the same time! Sylvia went to spend two weeks with her parents whilst Stuart was on holiday from Heversham Grammar School where he boarded and helped me to remove it.

I had closed the shop for two weeks so that I could try to get our home in reasonable shape for living in before Sylvia came back from her parents. So it was non-stop work in an effort to complete it all. After we'd removed the wooden chalet, barrow loads of earth had to be removed. I can't remember how many, we stopped counting after fifty. By the end of the two weeks everything had been achieved, inner foundations, supporting walls and floors completed, now the slates could be fixed on before the winter, as we certainly didn't want any more floods. I think Stuart was glad to get back to school although his help had been invaluable.

When Sylvia returned she couldn't believe how big it appeared inside, but of course when comparing it with the small amount of space we'd been used to, it must have seemed like a palace. Although we used Thermalite wall blocks they still required plastering. It was nevertheless a very satisfying scene, at least now I was halfway there and I could take a little more time on finishing it off.

It was Christmas Eve when the carpet was laid in the lounge, we'd had it stored at the shop for twelve months or more and now the room had been finished completely. We felt that at last we could relax a little. The other rooms would be completed in turn. The roof was finished, which was a great relief and the outside walls required pebble dashing. In just nine months the basic work was now complete and I was looking forward to getting on with all the finishing off bits, joinery, plastering and decorating, which of course was more in my own line of work.

Over the next three years, everything had been completed including the pebble dashing; crazy paved surrounding paths and outbuildings etc. I think that once you've made your mind to take on this kind of commitment you have to stay with it one hundred per cent, otherwise the work will drag on forever and a day, and become a burden. I was very fortunate that I'd had enough energy and resolve to see it through, for me it had become a very enjoyable and satisfying hobby, more than just a job of work. Of course it does help if you have an interested and understanding wife to help and support you, otherwise the task would have been quite impossible!

After eleven years in 1981 we decided to sell the shop in Kendal and enjoy a little more freedom. All the travelling to and fro, twice a day, six days a week to a busy shop had been a very enjoyable time, but very tying, and now it was time for a change. We sold it to Mr Ivan Bradbury (Dennis's brother) who used to own the Steak House on South Road, Kendal.

After a short spell relaxing, I would begin again doing the job I liked doing best – decorating! I was just fifty-five years old and with another ten years at least to go before even thinking about retirement. Cec was fifty-seven and of course still busy with his work, so it was inevitable that we should help each other on certain jobs just as before. Dennis Bradbury, with whom I'd been in partnership for nine years after returning from Canada, had also come up to the Lake District. He had been dad's last apprentice when I was conscripted during the war, so many times we would combine forces and work together just as we had done in the early post war years.

Many decorators in those days would leave a record of when the work had been carried out and also their names. Teddy would always draw around his scissors and papering brush on the chimney breast, add his name and date when it was done, before papering over. Many times when we were working together we uncovered records of his work done many years before, possibly not as common these days. It was a very interesting discovery for me when two workmen found a piece of wood with my brother Ellis's name on it, where it had lain untouched for almost sixty years. It was discovered on a ceiling beam during renovations in Mr Charlton's holiday cottage next to Lound Cottage. The lady who lived there, Mrs Caldwell, has since moved to Low Ludderburn, where Arthur Ransom and Amy Johnson's aunt lived. Before the war Mr Caldwell won the 'Brain of Cumbria Award' some years before he died, so the cottage has certainly had its share of famous people.

Mrs Caldwell kindly gave me the piece of wood that she had kept and wrote the following 'It will have more meaning and cherished memories for your family than obviously it would for me!' She was quite right of course. Ellis had died whilst serving in the RAF five years after leaving this memento. The piece of wood, probably a wedge of some sort, was two inches (5 cm) by one (2.5 cm) and eighteen inches (46 cm) in length.

Chapter Twenty-two

From Grenades to Strange but True!

In the early 1980s Stuart had left Heversham Grammar School and was now living at home, enjoying the country life as we all did. Gillian was still living in Kendal with David and they now had a daughter Louise and two young sons, Clarke and Curtis.

Stuart started his working days in Grizedale Forest training to be a lumberjack. Outdoor life was the major attraction and his hobbies were motorbike trials, fishing, walking, in fact anything to do with the outdoors and he was happy. So when his Uncle Trevor (Cec's youngest son) came over one day and invited him to go bottle hunting he was off like a shot.

Our son Stuart felling trees in Grizedale Forest in 1983

I suppose the lure of finding old artefacts from the past attracts many people and I suppose the best places to find them are the places where our predecessors have discarded them, their private tips, and that is where they went, to the cottage tip, over the wall and into the wood, no doubt digging down deep.

However, they came back with a little more than they had bargained for, not quite sure what it was and not having seen one before they brought it back to show me. Fortunately they hadn't tampered with it the pin and lever was still intact, it was a hand grenade! The last one I'd seen myself and had to use in training was in 1944 at Redford Barracks, in Edinburgh, where I'd completed my preliminary training.

I could hardly believe that someone would even contemplate fetching one home as a wartime souvenir and simply throw it on a tip, knowing how lethal they are. The grenade was placed in the centre of the field and covered by a bucket. The police were informed, who in turn passed this information on to the Bomb Disposal Squad, and we were told it would be some time during the afternoon before they arrived as they were based in Liverpool.

Whilst waiting, my thoughts went back to another incident that happened many years before at Lound Cottage, during the first year we came up to the Lake District. I was only four years old at the time, mother had always wanted a flower garden of her own, and the only place for one, was a small area at the top of the steps to the outside toilet which stretched about fifteen or sixteen feet (4-5 metres) to the end of the cottage, wall and about as wide.

My older brothers started to clear all the bushes and shrub, which had been neglected for quite some time whilst I watched on. Mother shouted up to them to come down for dinner, and with one final heave they managed to pull up quite a large bush that had grown up alongside the cottage wall. She shouted again, 'To come and get it!' They all did, leaving me on my own.

I can still remember going over to the hole against the cottage wall and scraping around with the trowel I had been holding, then uncovering a partially rusted cigarette tin with something inside. I managed to open it, probably hoping it was full of pennies but a few long shapes fell out, which I picked up and put back in the box.

I was sitting near the top of the stone steps happily using them as chisels to carve my initials in the stone when Archie wandered over from the cottage door and asked me what I was doing and what I was using. Then as he came up the steps he grabbed the stone out of my hand and all my chisels too then ran down the steps and into the cottage, with me chasing after him yelling, 'To give them back!' Needless to say they didn't.

It took a long time for mum and dad to calm me down but I of course never did get my chisels back, they were in fact six Army rifle bullets from the First World War. It was probably also a souvenir that someone had later buried for safety reasons and later a bush had been planted. At that time it was only twelve years after the Armistice had been signed.

However getting back to Trevor and Stuart, when the Bomb Squad did arrive it proved to be a First World War grenade, so it had lain there for around sixty-five years undisturbed, until that day but it was still just as lethal after all that time according to the Bomb Squad. It certainly went off with a bang!

It's very strange when things happen that can't really be explained, like dad, I always believed in logic, so I would have to see things for myself before believing in anything, but nevertheless some things happen that defy credibility.

Some years ago in the late 1980s Louise, my granddaughter, asked my wife to go with her to the Spiritual Hall, Appleby Road, Kendal (above NFU) one Saturday evening. So I drove her into town where they met for their spiritual evening. Then later when it was over, I picked my wife up again and we drove home. On the way I asked her what had happened, 'Oh, nothing much!' she replied. It was an older gentleman speaking and he was asking me a lot of things that didn't seem to make any sense. 'Like what?' I asked. 'Oh, well!' she answered, he asked me, 'Did I know of an old cottage where the leg of a bed went through the floor into the room below?' This I couldn't believe! So she repeated it again I said, 'You said, no! 'That really did happen.' I told her about the incident many years ago in Lound Cottage when we were small children. Unfortunately my wife and Louise knew nothing of this and had answered no to many of the questions they'd been asked but in fact they made a great deal of sense to me.

However they decided they would pay a second visit the following Saturday, as a younger man from Preston was coming to the Spiritual Hall and from all accounts he was very good so I drove my wife in again to meet Louise as before. But we waited and waited, right up until the last second before the meeting was due to start, my wife had wanted me to go in with her but I had refused each time she'd asked, then when I realized Louise wasn't coming, to keep the peace I finally gave in, on the understanding that we took a place right at the back of the hall, which was absolutely packed.

There were just two seats left so I slid down in mine as inconspicuously as possible, and my thoughts were, that with so many people here, it would be quite impossible for him to select either of us for a spiritual contact. After the opening introduction, the young man who happened to be a male nurse came forward to the front of the stage and proceeded to give a talk about 'Aids'. This lasted quite a while and I was beginning to get a little drowsy, when suddenly he gently clapped his hands, and said, 'Well I think I'd better get on with what I've come for, could I have the attention of the lady at the back row there?' And pointed directly to my wife.

Of course everyone looked around, we were the last in and my wife was the first chosen out of all these people, I felt quite embarrassed. He then went on to say, 'Please do not offer any other information to my questions other than, yes or no, or people may get the impression that I'm trying to lead you on.' After the first two questions relating to my wife's relatives to which both answers were 'yes', he suddenly said, 'Oh! I'm sorry but I think I should be addressing the lady sitting in front of you. Could you sit down and the lady in front stand up?' So we thought that was that but as he asked the lady in front certain names to which she answered 'no' to each time, it became obvious that he was right the first time. Every name he mentioned and every description was so exact and to the point that I could feel the hair bristling on the back of my head, how could he be so specific.

It was then that my wife and I looked at each other in disbelief. Then we both raised our arms together and my wife said to him, 'I'm sorry to intrude but we think it is me you should be addressing.' I think he must have felt a little relieved when we intervened because all the answers had been 'no' up until then. So the lady in front sat down and my wife stood up again, after that the answer to each question was 'yes.' I was astounded with the accuracy of the names, happenings and descriptions that came flowing out. It was uncanny I just couldn't believe it, no ifs or buts, it was if he'd known all my wife's relations personally, how could this be?

When my wife sat down she was quite shaken with the accuracy of all the things he had told her, and I have to admit so was I, had I not witnessed it all myself I would never have believed it. I was even more stunned with what was about to follow. When Sylvia sat down the young man put his hand to his forehead for a few seconds then turned around and said, 'Would the gentleman sitting next to the lady I have just spoken with stand up please?'

This was something I had not expected at all, I was feeling even more embarrassed with every one looking round and was still trying to take in the things he had said to my wife, so his next words came as a complete shock to me when he said, 'I have three gentlemen figures standing with me. Two of them appear to be in RAF uniform. Do you know of them?' I was completely stunned for a few seconds, and then I answered, 'Yes!'

I don't know what I was thinking when he followed up with, 'I have the name Harry for one. Is that correct?' I answered, 'No!' Sylvia tugged my coat and whispered, 'Your Sonny!' How could I make such a mistake he was my eldest brother, I'd never called him Harry, but I quickly corrected myself and said, 'I'm sorry, yes I do!' I think by now all my hair must have been standing on end. When I'd agreed to come into the meeting I had never expected anything like this to happen.

Then to cap it all, he said, 'There is also a young child figure standing here with them, would you know who this is?' For a second I was taken aback then I realised this must be Sybil the sister I never knew. She had passed away a few years before I was born at the age of five, so I answered, 'Yes.' He also mentioned mother and father and that they were all here in spirit form to wish us well. I really couldn't believe all this, he didn't know me and I didn't know him. Yet all this intimate information had been revealed, he couldn't have been reading my mind I was sure of that, because practically everything he had told me wasn't in my mind until he mentioned them.

Then as if to further convince me of their presence he said, 'They tell me that you recently had correspondence from Australia' then he hesitated for a second or two and said, 'but it could be America, I'm a little unsure about which country.' This was absolutely incredible I have no friends or relations in either Australia or America and yet in the previous week I had received two letters, one from Australia and one from America, these were the only two letters I had ever received from these countries and I have not received any since. I did of course answer, 'Yes, from both countries!'

Then he finished off by saying that the health problems I'd been having relating to my stomach, although uncomfortable at times, I should not worry too much about it. In fact I had been attending hospital for stomach problems at the time. I was very relieved to sit down again after all that. It was almost as if I'd been drawn to the Spiritual Hall that night and why did my granddaughter not turn up after making arrangements with my wife. If she had, I most certainly would not have gone in to the meeting, all these questions nagged in my mind.

Mother was a spiritual medium herself and so after this had happened I thought about many of the little incidents that had occurred when we were children back home, I remembered the table, that mother had got one of my elder brothers to paint a circle of white letters on. Then whenever dad was out, the cover was pulled off and a quick séance was held with friends or neighbours. An upturned glass was used to spell out the names of past on spirits and I would listen to the familiar sliding of the glass over the table top as it spelled out the names and messages of their friends and relations on the other side. Then whenever dad appeared the cover was quickly replaced but I knew that dad knew, although he always pretended he didn't.

I remember too when I was quite young mother had talked about her Indian spirit on the other side on a few occasions, then one day when I came into the house I saw this dark figure with a black moustache and beard, standing there, he looked so impressive with his immaculate green silk turban. I had never seen an Indian person before and thought at first it must be her Indian guide but then I looked on the couch and saw that he was trying to sell her silken ware.

Then on another occasion when I was sixteen I came home from the cinema one Saturday evening to find mother, Audrey and a family friend who was staying for the weekend whilst dad was away, sitting round a little coffee table trying to make contact with someone on the other side, so I joined them but nothing happened in spite of 'Is there anyone there? Three knocks for 'yes' and two knocks for 'no', routine. I said I would believe it all if I could see the table rise in the air, so mother had us all place our fingers on the table with everyone's fingers and thumbs joined together.

I had made the little table at school from softwood so it wouldn't be too heavy to raise but again in spite of all our efforts, nothing at all happened, so in the end I went to bed, mother and Audrey said, 'It was because I didn't believe in spiritualism!' I remember mother saying, 'Some day you may find out for yourself.'

Other almost forgotten incidents then came flying back to me, when after the war I'd been working with Sonny and somehow we'd got onto talking about Charlie our brother who'd been torpedoed. They were of course in business together and Sonny was telling me about how they'd sold their motorbikes and bought two three-wheeled Raleigh cars so they could pull a trailer for the ladders and materials. They'd also made a streamlined looking trailer, then painted them all blue, his was called 'Blue Streak' and Charlie's 'Blue Flash!'

I'd ridden in them myself on one or two occasions so I knew about them. I suppose they must have attracted many potential customers whenever they travelled through town. But as we spoke about Charlie and the time he came home on his last embarkation leave I said, I know he was very upset, when he was leaving our house, not the cheerful carefree Charlie he'd always been, it wasn't like him at all. Sonny was silent for quite a while, and then when he spoke, he made me promise not to tell anyone what had happened, and I haven't until now. He went on to say that the day he was due to go back from his embarkation leave, Charlie came into their workshop at the top of the street where they both lived, he was very upset about going back, then as he carried on telling me, Sonny himself faltered and I could see the tears welling in his eyes as he recalled that last day.

Sonny and Charlie were both very close, they did everything together just as Cec and myself did, and of course Archie and Ellis too, we all seemed to attach ourselves in that way, probably it was because we were of the same age groups and had gone to school together, so I knew what Sonny was feeling at that moment. After a while, Sonny told me what had happened, when Charlie came into the workshop that morning, he said, it was plain to see he was very upset and wanted to tell me something yet he kept holding it in, but finally he told me. It seemed that Charlie had had a strong premonition that he wasn't coming back and that this was the last day he would ever see any of his family again. A lump came into my throat whilst Sonny was telling me all this and then Sonny went on to say I tried to tell him it was just a bad dream he'd had but Charlie said, 'Oh no, it wasn't a dream it was much more than that, it was real.' There was no way I could console him, he wasn't afraid to go, it was just the thought of never seeing his wife, two sons and all his family ever again, it was more than he could bear.

When Sonny told me this I knew how Charlie must have felt when he came to see us to for the last time, and now I knew the reason why, I've never told anyone this, Sonny said, 'I didn't want mother and dad to know, so promised him I wouldn't either, but it was rather strange when a year or two later Sonny asked me had I mentioned this to anyone? I told him, 'No, I've never spoken about it at all,' which I hadn't. Then Sonny said, 'Well he went to the cottage last weekend and mother had said to him, 'You know!' Charlie knew he would never come back again, he'd had premonition.

We were the only two that knew this, and we both wondered how she'd known too but as Madge would say, 'One never knows does one? And when one does, one is never sure is one?' As I said at the beginning of this chapter some things cannot be explained but after experiencing all these happenings maybe mother was right after all. Was the Spiritual Hall incident designed to convince me that her belief was genuine? Then I recalled what mother had said, 'One day you may find out for yourself!'

Chapter Twenty-three

Retirement and memories!

Recently in 2002, I decided to visit Blakeholme and take a picture or two of the bay where the chalet was first situated before the Second World War. I'd never been there since my last wartime holiday with Roy and Arthur in 1943, that was fifty-nine years ago.

When I arrived at the entrance to open the gate, my mind went back to the times over seventy years ago when Cec and I would take turns to stand on the running boards of dad's car holding on with arms locked around the open window stanchions, then as we approached each gate we would eagerly jump off to open and shut them.

As I reached the farmhouse I was quite surprised to see that it hadn't altered one little bit, or the shippons to the right, it was just the same picture we would expect to see in the 1930s. The site manager was most obliging when I'd explained to him my reason for coming. 'It's all yours,' he said, 'the site's closed anyway for the winter season. So I got back into the car wondering how much the bay itself had changed, a couple of gates more to open and there it was, not a soul about, but it was mid-week and the end of the season. This was perfect, although the day was a little dark and I wondered whether my photographs would show clearly enough the bay where we had spent so many happy childhood days.

The site manager was quite right I did have it all to myself so I was not distracted by the noise of speedboats or the bustling of people and cars moving around. I parked the car in the very spot where the little wooden chalet had been to the right hand side of the barn, as seen from the lake, which now had been developed into four holiday flats.

I climbed up the wooden stairway to the top flat hoping to take a panoramic view of the whole bay as it would have been observed from the chalet but unfortunately the vision was obscured by trees that had been allowed to take over, along most of the shore line except for an opening where two wooden jetties had been constructed, reaching out some distance into the bay and I could see a few small motor cruisers anchored to their moorings here and there.

In spite of these extra additions over the years the bay itself had not changed or lost its magnetism, just as we had always been attracted to it when we were young, it was still being enjoyed by all the people who had caravans hidden around in the next little glade alongside the bay itself. But for this particular day, I had it all to myself and I was thankful for that, as I wandered around the whole stretch of the shoreline taking snaps.

Whilst I was taking the photos my thought flooded back to all the wonderful times we'd spent on this sheltered little bay and how lucky we were to have had elder brothers and sisters to look after us, and also caring parents to provide it all. I suppose when you're younger these things are taken for granted, but now there's just Audrey who lives in Cleveleys, Jean in St. Anne's and myself left. I realise just how fortunate our lives have been compared to others. Cec had a stroke and died on the 9th May 2001, he was seventy-seven.

I remember, Jimmy (the cobbler) visited us at the cottage after the war, riding on his motorcycle, with his wife in the sidecar and that was the last I saw of Jimmy. Likewise Arthur visited us, he was now married and had a restaurant somewhere in the Midlands. Arthur died in the 1980s. I have fond memories of them both.

Teddy, dad's faithful friend and employee, who could quite easily have doubled for Fred Astaire (American film star – renowned for his dancing) told me of his early years when he started work at twelve years old as a half-timer, going to school each morning then to work in the afternoon. He used to smoke 'thirty Woodbine (cigarettes) a day'. He never married and except for his war service worked for dad until he retired. He had a heart attack when he was sixty-three and sadly died in his seventies.

People and times just memories, but 'oh so clear and dear!' I retired from decorating recently. We sold our lovely house in the Winster Valley and moved to a more convenient flat in Milnthorpe in 1996. I am enjoying my retirement with Sylvia and my family living nearby. Our daughter Gillian and husband David live at Crook, just north of Kendal, and have one daughter, Louise and two sons, Clarke and Curtis. Our son Stuart and wife, Taslima live in Kendal and have two sons, Aaron and Blake. I have twenty-eight nieces and nephews, five grandchildren and two great-grandchildren. I hope they will all enjoy their lives as much as I have done.